NEW DIRECTIONS FOR STUDENT SERVICES

Margaret J. Barr, *Texas Christian University*
EDITOR-IN-CHIEF

M. Lee Upcraft, *The Pennsylvania State University*
ASSOCIATE EDITOR

Affirmative Action on Campus

Joseph G. Ponterotto
Fordham University

Diane E. Lewis
Fordham University

Robin Bullington
University of Houston

EDITORS

Number 52, Winter 1990

JOSSEY-BASS INC., PUBLISHERS
San Francisco

AFFIRMATIVE ACTION ON CAMPUS .
Joseph G. Ponterotto, Diane E. Lewis, Robin Bullington (eds.)
New Directions for Student Services, no. 52
Margaret J. Barr, Editor-in-Chief
M. Lee Upcraft, Associate Editor

Microfilm copies of issues and articles are available in 16mm and 35mm,
as well as microfiche in 105mm, through University Microfilms Inc., 300
North Zeeb Road, Ann Arbor, Michigan 48106.

LC 85-644751   ISSN 0164-7970   ISBN 1-55542-816-9

NEW DIRECTIONS FOR STUDENT SERVICES is part of The Jossey-Bass
Higher and Adult Education Series and is published quarterly by Jossey-
Bass Inc., Publishers (publication number USPS 449-070). Second-class
postage paid at San Francisco, California, and at additional mailing
offices. Postmaster: Send address changes to Jossey-Bass Inc., Publishers,
350 Sansome Street, San Francisco, California 94104.

EDITORIAL CORRESPONDENCE should be sent to the Editor-in-Chief,
Margaret J. Barr, Sadler Hall, Texas Christian University, Fort Worth,
Texas 76129.

Cover photograph by Wernher Krutein/PHOTOVAULT © 1990.

Printed on acid-free paper in the United States of America.

CONTENTS

6. Affirmative Action on Campus: Making It Work
Robert D. Brown, J. Manuel Casas, Doris J. Wright

Three student development experts present innovative and creative ideas about intensified affirmative action. The important roles of professional organizations, the private sector, and campus endowments are highlighted.

Key points are summarized, and additional sources of information are annotated.

EDITORS' NOTES

Affirmative action policies exist in most colleges and universities in the United States. Inspired by social, moral, philosophical, and legal imperatives, higher education institutions have been engaged in affirmative action efforts for more than twenty years. A systematic review of enrollment and retention data, however, indicates that progress with respect to increasing racial/ethnic minority representation on campus has been slow at best.

Women, despite significant educational enrollment and achievement gains, and although they now constitute the numerical majority on campuses, are still subjected to a campus climate that is often sexist, confining, and limiting. Other minority groups (such as persons with disabilities and elderly people) continue the struggle for equal educational access and opportunity.

Of particular concern to us—and the primary focus of this volume—is the status of racial/ethnic minority groups on predominantly white campuses. Demographic trends ensure that this collective group will represent our population's numerical majority within eighty years. Although modest gains with regard to educational access and retention have been made with some racial/ethnic minority groups, their representation overall on college campuses has not kept pace with their rapidly increasing numbers in society.

The implications of the data reviewed in this volume are significant. First, as racial/ethnic minority groups grow in number, and as the white majority decreases in proportional representation, many tuition-dependent colleges that have relied on enrollment of traditional students will face financial crisis. Second, the economic stability and leadership of our nation will be compromised as increasing numbers of citizens fail to realize their educational potential. Third, as the schism between the "haves" and the "have nots" widens along racial and ethnic lines, racial polarization, segregation, and conflict may intensify, both within and beyond campus walls.

Although most administrators have a sense of affirmative action issues, few fully understand the intention, meaning, scope, and implications of the policy. A major reason why affirmative action efforts have often failed is that not all campus personnel are committed to and involved in the process. For good reason, many individuals—both from the majority group and from minority groups—have mixed feelings about the justification and long-term benefits of affirmative action policy.

The major purpose of this volume is to present a condensed yet comprehensive overview of affirmative action issues on campus. The goal is to provide the reader with a basic understanding of the policy, so that informed decisions regarding whether and how to support the policy can be made. Student affairs administrators, given their responsibility for student development, must be at the forefront in implementing affirmative action ideals and goals, if the policy is to succeed.

Chapter One introduces the purpose and goals of affirmative action and profiles the groups covered by affirmative action policy. Significant demographic trends are noted, and varying perspectives on the need for affirmative action are presented. The chapter closes with ten questions about the student administrator's role in affirmative action. The questions serve as a cognitive map to guide the reader through the remaining chapters.

In Chapter Two, four major philosophical foundations of affirmative action are explored, and the origins of the so-called race-conscious and color-blind approaches to affirmative action are discussed. The chapter closes with an exercise designed to help student affairs units explore this controversial topic.

Chapter Three highlights the complex legal issues surrounding various aspects of affirmative action policy. Key laws and statutory provisions are highlighted, and recent Supreme Court cases are systematically examined. General as well as specific legal guidelines are presented, to assist administrators in their affirmative action planning.

In Chapter Four, national data on racial/ethnic minorities and women, in society and at all student levels of higher education, are presented. The chapter examines the campus climate for these groups and outlines specific steps that can be taken to facilitate a culturally pluralistic campus atmosphere.

Chapter Five, paralleling Chapter Four in scope and intent, focuses on data examining the current status of racial/ethnic minority and women administrators and faculty at all levels in higher education. The importance of a welcoming campus climate is again highlighted, and specific recommendations for recruiting culturally diverse faculty and administrators are presented.

In Chapter Six, three nationally distinguished student development experts present their perspectives on directions for affirmative action policy. Robert D. Brown discusses the important role that professional associations can play in fostering a more culturally pluralistic atmosphere on campus and in the profession. J. Manuel Casas shows that if affirmative action is to be successful in the long run, all segments of society must be involved. Doris J. Wright closes the chapter with an in-depth discussion of how student affairs educators must plan creatively and proactively to be ready for the challenges of higher education in the 1990s.

Chapter Seven concludes this volume with a brief summary of key points expressed throughout. Carefully selected sources of information are also abstracted for the interested administrator.

We end these notes with an expression of our appreciation for those who significantly helped the development and preparation of this volume. First, our four contributing authors must be thanked: Lindsay J. Lewis, our legal expert, who in Chapter Three helps us understand a complex legal issue; and Robert D. Brown, J. Manuel Casas, and Doris J. Wright, contributors to

Chapter Six, who offer unique and creative perspectives on affirmative action interventions. Others who helped by reading and commenting on early drafts or by tracking down difficult-to-find statistics are Ingrid Grieger of Iona College, Abigail Harris and Marian Mythen of Fordham University, John M. Ponterotto of Integrated Resources, Inc., Louis D. Ponterotto of Sewanhaka High School, and Frederick J. Ponterotto of the United States Postal Service. Finally, we thank Margaret J. Barr and M. Lee Upcraft, the series editors, for their encouragement, constructive feedback, and guidance during every phase of this volume's development.

Joseph G. Ponterotto
Diane E. Lewis
Robin Bullington
Editors

Joseph G. Ponterotto is associate professor of counseling and counseling psychology in the Division of Psychological and Educational Services, Graduate School of Education, Fordham University–Lincoln Center, New York.

Diane E. Lewis is a doctoral student in counseling psychology at Fordham University.

Robin Bullington is a doctoral student in counseling psychology at the University of Houston.

As the demographic makeup of the United States shifts dramatically,
affirmative action issues on campus will become increasingly
important.

Affirmative Action: Current Status and Future Needs

Joseph G. Ponterotto

The term *affirmative action* is often used on college campuses, yet few student affairs administrators fully understand the meaning, legality, and implications of the concept. Given the recent conservative precedents established by the Supreme Court, and when we consider projected economic and political conditions in this country and acknowledge recent and projected demographic trends among the U.S. population, it is evident that universities will have to devote intensified efforts to affirmative action if their campuses are to reflect a culturally pluralistic learning environment. Affirmative action policy is controversial, and it is important that student affairs administrators have a firm grasp of the legal aspects of affirmative action. They must also know their own personal views of the mechanisms and goals of the policy.

This chapter introduces affirmative action policy and raises some important issues with respect to the administrator's role in the university's affirmative action efforts. The chapter is organized into five major sections, which cover the purpose and focus of affirmative action, the current status of minorities in higher education, the changing demographics of minority groups, the consequences of minority underrepresentation in higher education, and the student affairs administrator's role in affirmative action.

Purpose and Focus of Affirmative Action

University-based affirmative action programs are designed to give minority-group members—primarily racial/ethnic minorities, women, persons with disabilities, and elderly people—greater access to and support in

NEW DIRECTIONS FOR STUDENT SERVICES, no. 52, Winter 1990 © Jossey-Bass Inc., Publishers

higher education. The ultimate goal of such programs is to enable these individuals, through educational achievement, to have greater access to socioeconomic (and concurrent social) opportunity and stability.

Affirmative action programs arose out of governmental and judicial decisions requiring efforts to remedy past and continuing discrimination based on sex and race (Ponterotto, Martinez, and Hayden, 1986). Sowell (1980) notes that the central goal of affirmative action is not only to eliminate instances of current discrimination but also to take *affirmative* steps to mitigate the long-term effects of past discrimination. On the college campus, affirmative action's ideals are translated into combating sexism and racism and taking active steps to facilitate the recruitment, retention, and social acceptance of minority-group members.

The targets of affirmative action efforts are the specific groups that historically have been the objects of discrimination. Decades of social, educational, and employment discrimination have hindered these groups with respect to social power and economic status. Collectively, we refer to these groups as *minorities*. By this term, we are referring not so much to numerical minorities as to minorities in terms of status, power, and influence. On the college campus, the power-dominant "majority" group is clearly white males (see Pearson, Shavlik, and Touchton, 1989); minority groups include racial/ethnic minorities (particularly blacks, Hispanics, Native Americans, and Asian Americans), women, persons with disabilities, and elderly people (generally defined as being sixty-five years old and older). The working definition of the term *minority* used throughout this volume parallels the one developed by Wirth (1945, p. 347): "a group of people who, because of physical or cultural characteristics, are singled out from others in the society in which they live for differential and unequal treatment, and who therefore regard themselves as objects of collective discrimination."

Current Status of Minorities in Higher Education

The United States has been described as a "highly technological and credential-oriented society, in which anyone possessing a bright analytical mind, hard-driving ambition, the finest technological resources, a college degree, and an edge on the market will succeed" (Wright, 1987b, p. 5). The American power structure highly values education, and there is a strong link between educational attainment and economic stability (Nettles, 1988b).

Because America has long been viewed as the land of opportunity, one would hope that all its citizens have equal access to and potential for success in higher education. Unfortunately, this ideal has never been realized. Nonwhite and nonmale persons continue to be highly underrepresented (that is, relative to their numbers in society) in the university power structure (for example, among top administrators and tenured faculty) and in a number of undergraduate and graduate programs. Racial/ethnic minorities, women, persons with disabilities, and elderly people have fought and continue to fight long, hard battles to become valued members of the college community (see Astin, 1982; Atkinson and Hackett, 1988; Atkinson, Morten, and Sue, 1989; Casas and Ponterotto, 1984; Danowitz Sagaria, 1988; Evans, 1985; Nettles, 1988b; Pearson, Shavlik, and Touchton, 1989; Pounds, 1987; Wright, 1987a).

Despite some efforts on the part of predominantly white institutions to redress the effects of past discrimination, through gender- and race-based affirmative action recruitment efforts, minority groups continue to be severely underrepresented at almost every level of higher education. Women, although they appeared in much larger numbers on college campuses in the 1980s, are still underrepresented in many of the higher-earning-potential programs, such as engineering and the physical sciences (women have, however, increased their numbers in medical and law schools; see Chapter Four). Moreover, in terms of tenured faculty appointments and administrative leadership, women continue to be underrepresented, relative to their general numbers on campus and in society (see Atkinson and Hackett, 1988; Chipman and Thomas, 1987; Evans, 1985). In terms of campus climate, there is no question that women continue to be targets of sexual harassment and violence (see Sherrill and Siegel, 1989).

The conditions for racial/ethnic minorities on campus are no better; in fact, they are probably worse than they are for women. Demographically, because of continued immigration trends and fertility rates in some racial/ethnic subgroups, people of color are increasing numerically at a much faster rate than the white population is (Davis, Haub, and Willette, 1988; Hodgkinson, 1985; Ponterotto and Casas, 1987). On college campuses, however, the numbers of racial/ethnic minority students, staff, and faculty have not kept pace with the growth of racial/ethnic minority groups in society (see Richardson and Bender, 1987; Wright, 1987b). Some writers have noted that, after initial growth rates that followed the civil rights movement of the 1960s and 1970s, the racial/ethnic minority student population on campus has actually decreased (Nettles, 1988a; Ponce, 1988; Pounds, 1987).

Persons with disabilities and elderly people also constitute minority groups on campus. These groups have received less attention in the higher education literature, and yet their exclusion from campus representation and leadership warrants close scrutiny with regard to affirmative action policy. Despite some progress in social attitudes toward these groups, the evidence indicates that they continue to be ignored, neglected, and confronted with discriminatory attitudes, both on and off campus (Atkinson and Hackett, 1988).

Minority Groups: Changing Demographics

Demographic patterns in the United States are changing quickly, and the pool of "traditional" college students—white, young-adult males—is shrinking rapidly (Hodgkinson, 1985). To fully understand the significance of current and future affirmative action efforts, it is essential that student affairs administrators have an accurate understanding of the demographic changes taking place in the United States.

In this section specifically, and throughout this volume generally, select and focused attention will be directed toward the four minority groups already named. Of the four groups, racial/ethnic minorities have received the most attention in the recent higher education literature (for example, Nettles, 1988b; Richardson and Bender, 1987; Wright, 1987b) and as the focus of special reports (for example, Commission on Minority Participation in Education and American Life, 1988). Our coverage of the minority groups will also reflect this weighted balance. Given the extremely rapid demographic growth of racial/ethnic minority populations, the recent reports of their declining educational achievement (Ponce, 1988) and its concurrent economic implications (Nettles, 1988b), and the recent upsurge of racial tension on campuses throughout the United States (Peoples, 1988), we believe that this group deserves the most comprehensive coverage. In no way, however, does our enhanced focus on racial/ethnic minority groups detract from the importance of increasing affirmative action vigilance with the other groups. The remaining portion of this section presents brief demographic profiles of each of the minority groups discussed here.

Women. Women currently constitute a slight majority in society (U.S. Bureau of the Census, 1988) and on college campuses (Astin, 1984; Evans, 1985; Pearson, Shavlik, and Touchton, 1989). Recent trends and predictions highlight the probability that, in the 1990s, an increasing proportion of adult "re-entry" students will be women (see Holliday, 1985). A major reason why adult women return to school is money. Tightening economic conditions, coupled with changes in the "traditional" family's makeup and more accepting attitudes toward working women, are influencing many women to enter the labor force (see Atkinson and Hackett, 1988; Holliday, 1985). By 1985, 60 percent of all women, 50 percent of married women, and 45 percent of mothers with preschool children were members of the labor force (Atkinson and Hackett, 1988; Hewlett, 1986). Betz and Fitzgerald (1987) project that, by 1990 or so, over 70 percent of all women will be working outside the home. Before entering the work force, many women will return to school. Student affairs administrators need to be aware of the changing status of women on campus, and they must be sensitive to the unique needs of and barriers to these students (see Danowitz Sagaria, 1988).

Elderly People. Because of the declining general birthrate and the increasing life-expectancy rate, the elderly population in the United States is increasingly rapidly. In 1982, the elderly population represented 11.6 percent of the total U.S. population; the elderly population is expected to comprise 19.5 percent by the year 2025 (Achenbaum, 1978; U.S. Bureau of the Census, 1983b). Atkinson and Hackett (1988) report that the total U.S. population grew 13.5 percent from 1970 to 1982, while the elderly group grew 34.3 percent. Demographers project that one-half of all college students by 1992 will be over the age of twenty-five, and 20 percent will be over thirty-five (Hodgkinson, 1985).

Despite their protection under civil rights laws, elderly people still face discrimination in society and on college campuses. As 1992 approaches and forced retirement is legally abolished, the elderly population on campus will grow, and the chances for intensified "ageism" will increase. Student affairs administrators are professionally and ethically responsible for their own and their staffs' affirmative action-based knowledge with respect to this group.

Persons with Disabilities. Atkinson and Hackett (1988) note that there is no clear consensus on what constitutes a disabled person. U.S. government agencies currently have no clear estimate of the actual number of disabled persons in the United States, although some figures are available. The U.S. Bureau of the Census (1983a) estimates that 13.1 million noninstitutionalized men and women between the ages of sixteen and twenty-five have had work disabilities (defined as mental or physical conditions of at least six months' duration, which prevent a person from working). These data also show that over 6 million noninstitutionalized persons had public-transportation handicaps in 1982. Bowe (1980) estimates that the disabled population in the United States is approximately 36 million, or roughly 15 percent of the total population. If one also considers "hidden" disabilities (such as learning disabilities), the numbers jump dramatically.

Despite their significant presence among the U.S. population as a whole, persons with disabilities represent fewer than 1 percent (not counting persons with learning disabilities) of students enrolled in colleges and universities (Seaquist, 1988). Evangelauf (1989) reports that only 15 percent of disabled high school graduates and dropouts enroll in vocational, two-year, or four-year college programs. Students and staff with physical disabilities do have special needs, and yet their academic and professional potential is as high as that of other students. Administrators must work toward making campuses more hospitable and welcoming for these individuals.

Racial/Ethnic Minorities. Racial/ethnic minority groups in the United States, particularly blacks and Hispanics, are growing at a much faster pace than the white population is. By 1980, the annual growth rate for whites was 0.06 percent, while comparable estimates for blacks and Hispanics were 1.8 percent and 6.1 percent, respectively (Malgady, Rogler, and Costantino, 1987). At present, the total minority population stands at approximately 20 percent of the U.S. population, and it is projected that this percentage will jump to 25 percent by the early 1990s (American Psychological Association, 1985). Longer-term projections estimate that by the year 2020, 91 million of the 265 million Americans will be of racial/ethnic minority status, representing over 34 percent of the total U.S. population (Hodgkinson, 1985). Within eighty years, racial/ethnic minorities will become the nation's numerical majority (Ponterotto and Casas, forthcoming).

The rapid demographic shift in the population is already evident in the nation's elementary school enrollments. By 1985, California's elementary school population was over 50 percent nonwhite. Texas schools are 46 percent racial/ethnic minority. Twenty-five states have public school populations that are more than 25 percent nonwhite, and all of our twenty-five largest city school systems have "minority majorities" (see Hodgkinson, 1985). Nationally, 20 percent of the school-age population was nonwhite by 1985; by the year 2000, the figure will be 33 percent, and by the year 2020, racial/ethnic minorities will comprise 39 percent of the total school-age population (Commission on Minority Participation in Education and American Life, 1988).

Clearly, an important concern of today's colleges and universities is that the great majority of this rapidly growing segment of our population does not attend college and complete baccalaureate degrees (Richardson and Bender, 1987). In 1986, 20.1 percent of whites over twenty-five years old had completed four or more years of college. The comparable rates for racial/ethnic minority groups were 10.9 percent for blacks and 8.4 percent for Hispanics (Commission on Minority Participation in Education and American Life, 1988). The attrition rates for blacks, Hispanics, and especially Native Americans are alarmingly high. (Educational achievement levels and attrition rates for racial/ethnic minorities are covered in more detail in Chapter Four.)

Consequences of Racial/Ethnic Minority Underrepresentation in Higher Education

The social and economic implications of a growing but marginally educated segment of the population are staggering and frightening. Recently, the American Council on Education and the Education Commission of the States jointly created the Commission on Minority Participation in Education and American Life, to study the current status of racial/ethnic minorities in education. The commission was formed in response to mounting concern over discouraging trends in the education of racial/ethnic minority citizens and the obvious implications for future national economic conditions. The commission's final report, commenting on the lack of racial/ethnic minorities' full participation in the American dream, says, "We have underestimated the depth and complexity of the situation, as well as the need for sustained institutional and governmental commitment. We also have found that some of the more difficult barriers to full participation by minority young people are not so obvious. An unacceptably large number conclude at an early age that education is not for them. Even among those who make it into four-year colleges and universities, attrition rates are unacceptably high. This calls for a new understanding and a more creative approach to the barriers to success faced by minority youth from kindergarten through graduate school" (Commission on Minority Participation in Education and American Life, 1988, p. v.). Referring to the widening gap between members of racial/ethnic minority groups and the majority population in such areas as education, employment, and income, the report comments (p. vii), "If we allow these disparities to continue, the United States inevitably will suffer a compromised quality of life and a lower standard of living. Social conflict will intensify. Our ability to compete in world markets will decline, our domestic economy will falter, our national security will be endangered. In brief, we will find ourselves unable to fulfill the promise of the American dream."

As national data are examined and projected educational achievement trends are clarified (see Chapter Four), the implications of racial/ethnic minorities' underrepresentation in higher education become more salient and obvious. If universities are someday to reflect the culturally pluralistic reality of the real world, then university administrators—from presidents to chief student affairs officers to directors of student services programs—must be personally involved in understanding, implementing, and ensuring the success of affirmative action policy on campus.

Student Affairs Administrators and Affirmative Action

What is the student affairs administrator's role in relation to the university's policy of and commitment to affirmative action? Most affirmative action experts would agree that student affairs professionals at all levels need to be more integrally involved in affirmative action efforts if these efforts are to be successful. Despite some efforts at recruiting and retaining minority students and staff, the status of minorities on campus has changed little in recent years. As Upcraft (1988, p. 42) comments, "Very few student affairs organizations have satisfied their commitment to hiring women, ethnic minorities, the disabled, and other categories of persons who are legally protected from discrimination. Even if women and minorities are in the organization, they are often in the lower levels."

How much policy and legal knowledge does the average student affairs administrator possess with regard to affirmative action? Most administrators are aware that their universities have affirmative action policies. Most feel pressure to recruit and hire more minorities for staff jobs. Most have a general sense of some civil rights laws and of frequently cited affirmative action cases, and most know that caution must be exercised in hiring and promoting, lest charges of discrimination or so-called reverse discrimination be brought against administrators and universities.

Despite student administrators' general knowledge of affirmative action policy, it would be fair to say that many are not fully aware of the purpose, goals, legality, and socioeconomic implications of affirmative action. The mechanisms of affirmative action are debatable and have evoked strong feelings, both for and against the policy (Ponterotto, Martinez, and Hayden, 1986). Clearly, not everyone is in favor of affirmative action, and nonsupporters include both majority and minority individuals. At the core of the affirmative action debate lie fundamental philosophical issues, and it is important that student affairs administrators think through their own philosophical positions on affirmative action. One's own emotional reaction or affective response to affirmative action goals and procedures must also be identified and processed.

For a student affairs administrator to effectively support the university's commitment to affirmative action and abide by affirmative action case law, she or he must possess a certain relevant knowledge base. Such a knowledge base would include the information necessary to respond confidently to the following questions:

1. What, specifically, is affirmative action? Is there one accepted and agreed-on definition?
2. What are the philosophical foundations of affirmative action? Are varying philosophical positions at the root of strong mixed feelings about affirmative action?
3. What is affirmative action, from a purely legal perspective? Which civil rights laws apply to affirmative action issues? What are my legal obligations to minority and majority students, in terms of potential discrimination and so-called reverse discrimination?
4. What affirmative action cases have recently been heard by the Supreme Court? What is the court's position on justifications for and proper implementation of affirmative action policy?
5. Have affirmative action efforts during the last decade been successful? Have universities improved their record of recruiting, admitting, supporting (academically and socially), and graduating racial/ethnic minority and women students?
6. Has affirmative action worked with respect to female and racial/ethnic minority faculty and staff? Have efforts in this vein been more or less successful than student-targeted affirmative action?
7. What specific strategies are effective in increasing the representation of racial/ethnic minorities on campus and creating a more culturally pluralistic academic environment?
8. How can student affairs staff work with their umbrella professional organizations to enhance the success of affirmative action policies?

9. What are some creative mechanisms for implementing affirmative action goals, both on and off campus?
10. *How do I feel* about affirmative action? Do I think it's necessary? Is it fair to all involved?

The remaining chapters of this volume attempt to provide the information necessary to answer these questions. Once the student affairs administrator can answer them, she or he will have a satisfactory understanding of affirmative action and will be able to take a personally comfortable and legally knowledgeable stand on affirmative action mechanisms and decisions.

References

Achenbaum, W. A. *Old Age in the New Land: The American Experience Since 1790.* Baltimore, Md.: Johns Hopkins University Press, 1978.

American Psychological Association. *Issues and Concerns Regarding the Preparation of Psychologists for Service and Research with Ethnic Minority Populations.* Washington, D.C.: American Psychological Association, 1985.

Astin, A. W. *Minorities in American Higher Education: Recent Trends, Current Prospects, and Recommendations.* San Francisco: Jossey-Bass, 1982.

Astin, A. W. "A Look at Pluralism in the Contemporary Student Population." *NASPA Journal,* 1984, *21* (3), 2–12.

Atkinson, D. R., and Hackett, G. (eds.). *Counseling Non-Ethnic Minorities.* Springfield, Ill.: Thomas, 1988.

Atkinson, D. R., Morten, G., and Sue, D. W. (eds.). *Counseling American Minorities: A Cross-Cultural Perspective.* (3rd ed.) Dubuque, Iowa: Brown, 1989.

Betz, N. E., and Fitzgerald, L. F. *The Career Psychology of Women.* Orlando, Fla.: Academic Press, 1987.

Bowe, F. *Rehabilitating America.* New York: Harper & Row, 1980.

Casas, J. M., and Ponterotto, J. G. "Profiling an Invisible Minority in Higher Education: The Chicana." *Personnel and Guidance Journal,* 1984, *62* (6), 349–353.

Chipman, S. F., and Thomas, V. G. "The Participation of Women and Minorities in Mathematical, Scientific, and Technical Fields." In E. Z. Rothkopf (ed.), *Review of Research in Education.* Washington, D.C.: American Educational Research Association, 1987.

Commission on Minority Participation in Education and American Life. *One-Third of a Nation.* Washington, D.C.: American Council on Education, Education Commission of the States, 1988.

Danowitz Sagaria, M. A. (ed.). *Empowering Women: Leadership Development Strategies on Campus.* New Directions for Student Services, no. 44. San Francisco: Jossey-Bass, 1988.

Davis, C., Haub, C., and Willette, J. L. "U.S. Hispanics: Changing the Face of America." In E. Acost-Belen and B. R. Sjostrom (eds.), *The Hispanic Experience in the United States: Contemporary Issues and Perspectives.* New York: Praeger, 1988.

Evangelauf, J. "Small Percentage of Disabled Youths Enroll in College, Study Finds." *Chronicle of Higher Education,* Apr. 19, 1989, p. A32.

Evans, N. J. (ed.). *Facilitating the Development of Women.* New Directions for Student Services, no. 29. San Francisco: Jossey-Bass, 1985.

Hewlett, S. A. *A Lesser Life: The Myth of Women's Liberation in America.* New York: Morrow, 1986.

Hodgkinson, H. L. *All One System: Demographics of Education, Kindergarten Through Graduate School.* Washington, D.C.: Institute for Educational Leadership, 1985.

Holliday, G. "Addressing the Concerns of Returning Women Students." In N. J. Evans (ed.), *Facilitating the Development of Women.* New Directions for Student Services, no. 29. San Francisco: Jossey-Bass, 1985.

Malgady, R. G., Rogler, L. H., and Costantino, G. "Ethnocultural and Linguistic Bias in Mental Health Evaluation of Hispanics." *American Psychologist,* 1987, 42 (3), 228–234.

Nettles, M. T. "Introduction: Contemporary Barriers to Black Student Equality in Higher Education." In M. T. Nettles (ed.), *Toward Black Undergraduate Student Equality in American Higher Education.* Westport, Conn.: Greenwood Press, 1988a.

Nettles, M. T. (ed.). *Toward Black Undergraduate Student Equality in American Higher Education.* Westport, Conn.: Greenwood Press, 1988b.

Pearson, C. S., Shavlik, D. L., and Touchton, J. G. (eds.). *Educating the Majority: Women Challenge Tradition in Higher Education.* New York: Macmillan, 1989.

Peoples, N. L. "Multiculturalism in the Postsecondary Setting." *Black Issues in Higher Education,* 1988, 5 (3), 52.

Ponce, F. Q. "Minority Student Retention: Historical Beginnings." In M. C. Terrell and D. J. Wright (eds.), *From Survival to Success: Promoting Minority Student Retention.* Washington, D.C.: National Association of Student Personnel Administrators, 1988.

Ponterotto, J. G., and Casas, J. M. "In Search of Multicultural Competence Within Counselor Education Programs." *Journal of Counseling and Development,* 1987, 65 (8), 430–434.

Ponterotto, J. G., and Casas, J. M. *Handbook of Racial/Ethnic Minority Counseling Research.* Springfield, Ill.: Thomas, in press.

Ponterotto, J. G., Martinez, F. M., and Hayden, D. C. "Student Affirmative Action Programs: A Help or Hindrance to Development of Minority Graduate Students?" *Journal of College Student Personnel,* 1986, 27 (4), 318–325.

Pounds, A. W. "Black Students' Needs on Predominantly White Campuses." In D. J. Wright (ed.), *Responding to the Needs of Today's Minority Students.* New Directions for Student Services, no. 38. San Francisco: Jossey-Bass, 1987.

Richardson, R. C., Jr., and Bender, L. W. *Fostering Minority Access and Achievement in Higher Education: The Role of Urban Community Colleges and Universities.* San Francisco: Jossey-Bass, 1987.

Seaquist, G. "Civil Rights and Equal Access: When Laws Apply—and When They Do Not." In M. J. Barr and Associates, *Student Services and the Law: A Handbook for Practitioners.* San Francisco: Jossey-Bass, 1988.

Sherrill, J. M., and Siegel, D. G. *Responding to Violence on Campus.* New Directions for Student Services, no. 47. San Francisco: Jossey-Bass, 1989.

Sowell, T. "*Weber* and *Bakke,* and the Presuppositions of Affirmative Action." *Wayne Law Review,* 1980, 26 (4), 1309–1336.

Upcraft, M. L. "Managing Staff." In M. L. Upcraft and M. J. Barr (eds.), *Managing Student Affairs Effectively.* New Directions for Student Services, no. 41. San Francisco: Jossey-Bass, 1988.

U.S. Bureau of the Census. *Labor Force and Other Characteristics of Persons with a Work Disability: 1982.* Current Population Reports, series P-23, no. 127. Washington, D.C.: U.S. Government Printing Office, 1983a.

U.S. Bureau of the Census. *Population Profile of the United States: 1982.* Current Population Reports, series P-23, no. 130. Washington, D.C.: U.S. Government Printing Office, 1983b.

U.S. Bureau of the Census. *Statistical Abstract of the United States: 1988.* (108th ed.) Washington, D.C.: U.S. Government Printing Office, 1988.

Wirth, L. "The Problem of Minority Groups." In R. Linton (ed.), *The Science of Man in World Crisis.* New York: Columbia University Press, 1945.

Wright, D. J. "Minority Students: Developmental Beginnings." In D. J. Wright (ed.), *Responding to the Needs of Today's Minority Students.* New Directions for Student Services, no. 38. San Francisco: Jossey-Bass, 1987a.

Wright, D. J. (ed.). *Responding to the Needs of Today's Minority Students.* New Directions for Student Services, no. 38. San Francisco: Jossey-Bass, 1987b.

Joseph G. Ponterotto is associate professor of counseling and counseling psychology in the Division of Psychological and Educational Services, Graduate School of Education, Fordham University–Lincoln Center, New York.

The affirmative action debate is rooted in disagreement about fundamental issues.

Affirmative Action: Definitions and Philosophy

Robin Bullington, Joseph G. Ponterotto

Writing about federal education policy, Salomone (1986, p. 15) observes, "It is well understood, although seldom stated, that public policy making operates within a given political ideology and draws from particular moral principles." Similarly, university policies on such matters as affirmative action are also influenced by the political and moral convictions of those who shape the policies. The role of philosopher may not be routinely included in the job description of a university administrator; nevertheless, those making decisions about affirmative action on campus and trying to answer the questions raised in Chapter One will sometimes face philosophical issues. These include equality, justice, and what makes a society good.

Today's student affairs officials, of course, are not the first to consider such matters. Fundamental philosophical conflict exists, both in the definition of affirmative action, evolving since the mid 1960s, and in the continuing debate over what affirmative action should mean and how it should be implemented. A brief review of these issues, in the context of the history and the long debate over affirmative action, should help the student affairs administrator examine or formulate her or his own position on this controversial subject.

Affirmative Action: Definition and History

A reporter (Greenhouse, 1989b, p. A18) recently defined *affirmative action* as "a broad, umbrella term, meaning different things to different people but generally covering a wide range of programs aimed at helping minorities,

NEW DIRECTIONS FOR STUDENT SERVICES, no. 52, Winter 1990 © Jossey-Bass Inc., Publishers

or, in some cases, women." This very general definition may be the only acceptable kind. While virtually no one disputes that governments, employers, and educational institutions should make special efforts to assist minorities, strong disagreement exists about what activities and programs are appropriate in this helping effort.

By the late 1960s, a debate was developing over affirmative action as former allies in the civil rights movement began to disagree about how to implement the provisions of landmark legislation passed in 1964 (Glazer, 1983). Although presidential executive orders had been issued from the 1940s through the 1960s and scattered efforts, state and private, had attempted to increase employment opportunities for blacks (Weiss, 1987), it was not until the Civil Rights Act of 1964 that the legislative and executive branches of the federal government joined in an effort to combat the national problem of harmful discrimination in education and employment.

The Civil Rights Act banned discrimination on the basis of an individual's race, sex, color, religion, or national origin and created the Equal Employment Opportunity Commission (EEOC) for enforcement. Comprehensive in scope, the legislation was applicable to discriminatory practices in voting, in places of public accommodation and public facilities, in employment, and in federally aided public education. Past or current intentional violators of the act would have to cease their illegal practices and could be subject to court-ordered affirmative action directives. Section 706 (g) (cited in Glazer, 1983, p. 162) provided that appropriate affirmative action "may include, but is not limited to, reinstatement or hiring of employees, with or without back pay, or any other equitable relief as the court deems appropriate."

Exactly what the new law required or prohibited in the pursuit of equal treatment and nondiscrimination—exactly what affirmative action meant—remained unclear. Weiss (1987, p. 48) observed that "by 1965 . . . federal civil rights directives had been issued which accepted the legitimacy of affirmative action without seeking to define it." Presidents Johnson, Nixon, and Carter were willing to use numerical hiring goals to comply with the law. During the Johnson administration, the Labor Department issued guidelines requiring large employers to submit written plans for affirmative action, including annually updated "goals and timetables for minority hiring" (Weiss, 1987, p. 50). The Nixon administration also required such plans from government contractors; it was this administration's affirmative action rules for government contractors that "made numerical affirmative action part of American life" ("True Affirmative Action," 1985, p. 4). For those doing business with the government, race became an employment consideration.

As presidential efforts to execute the law continued, the courts began to interpret it. "Women, linguistic minorities, and the handicapped— groups historically underrepresented in the majoritarian political process—

began to make an end-run around the legislative branch and carry their claims before the federal courts" (Salomone, 1986, p. 7). These lawsuits reflected a conviction among some in the civil rights movement: the discrimination that affirmative action should address was not so much a product of evil employers' actions as a reflection of a more socially pervasive phenomenon that required a broad remedy. Beer (1985, p. 17) observes that such a view assumes that "racial discrimination is the most important reason for the underrepresentation of black Americans in prestigious and lucrative occupations."

Some of the cases concerning discrimination and affirmative action found their way to the Supreme Court, which has issued rulings characterized by one writer as "complicated, contradictory, and qualified" (Brimelow, 1986, p. 11). Weiss (1987, p. 49) calls the Supreme Court decisions "increasingly liberal" (nevertheless, the reader should consider the Supreme Court's 1988 term, discussed in detail in Chapter Three), and Sowell (1980, p. 1336) believes that the court's role in defining affirmative action has indicated a movement "from democracy to a judicial *ad hocracy.*"

As the judiciary's role in defining affirmative action grew, so did disagreement among the civil rights advocates who had worked together for antidiscrimination laws. All could agree that an end to discrimination was the goal; Glazer (1983, p. 161) defines this as "the achievement of a society in which ethnic and racial affiliation did not affect important individual decisions (whom to employ, or rent or sell a house to, and the like)." But opinions on how best to achieve the goal divided former allies into two groups: those advocating a color-blind (or simple nondiscrimination) approach, and those supporting a race-conscious, preferential-treatment initiative.

Affirmative Action Debate: Color-Blind Versus Race-Conscious

Color-blind proponents, generally regarded as the more conservative, supported vigorous and sustained efforts by employers and institutions to develop and publicize nondiscriminatory hiring and admissions policies; to advertise in media likely to be seen by minority candidates; to recruit in high schools, colleges, and neighborhoods populated by minorities; and to offer special training for minorities (Glazer, 1983; Sowell, 1980). The Reagan administration exemplified this color-blind approach: one Department of Justice attorney (Mann, 1987, p. 6) noted that it pursued "traditional" affirmative action remedies, including "affirmative outreach, recruitment, and training programs designed to attract to the pool of qualified applicants increased numbers of [racial/ethnic] minorities and women able to compete for vacant positions."

Those supporting this approach are most interested in equalizing opportunities to compete for education and employment, and they tend to accept that inequalities in achievement and income will continue to exist. It is part of an American belief (or tradition) expressed as early as 1832 by Andrew Jackson: "Equality of talents, of education, or of wealth cannot be produced by human institutions. . . . If [government] would confine itself to equal protection, and . . . shower its favors alike on the high and the low, the rich and the poor, it would be an unqualified blessing" (cited in Hofstadter, 1977, p. 60).

But a literal lack of discrimination seemed inadequate to the race-conscious proponents interested in expanding civil rights for the educationally and economically disadvantaged. While approving of efforts to expand minority recruitment and training, this faction of the affirmative action debate saw these measures as inadequate to the task of achieving better education and employment for minorities. The race-conscious group advocated an approach variously called *preferential treatment, reverse discrimination,* or *affirmative discrimination* (Dreyfuss and Lawrence, 1979; Fullinwider, 1980; Glazer, 1983). This allows or encourages consideration of an applicant's minority status in admissions, hiring, promotion, and retention decisions, and it emphasizes the attainment of established numerical goals, or quotas.

Recognizing that racial preference may be criticized (see the next section, on philosophical foundations), advocates of preferential treatment defend these policies as temporarily necessary to overcome the harsh legacy of legal discrimination. Krauthammer (1985, p. 10) notes, "While color-blindness may be a value, remedying centuries of discrimination is a higher value." In a similar vein, Justice Blackmun has observed, "In order to get beyond racism, we must first take account of race" (cited in Greenhouse, 1989b, p. A18).

Whether opponents or supporters of preferential treatment hold the upper hand in efforts to define affirmative action depends largely on the tone and direction of court decisions (to be discussed at length in Chapter Three). As Glazer (1983, p. 177) observes, "The judiciary has shaped the present policies; it is also capable of revising them." Beneath continuing judicial ambiguity lies fundamental disagreement about "some of the most basic questions about social justice and human rights" (Fullinwider, 1980, p. 8). It is essential that the student affairs administrator have a basic understanding of these questions, so that he or she can facilitate discussion and exploration of affirmative action.

Philosophical Considerations

It is doubtful that university administrators will be able to take a confident and effective stand on affirmative action issues unless they are knowledgeable about the philosophical arguments surrounding the affirmative action debate. These arguments, while interrelated, can be divided into four broad categories: social utility, distributive justice, compensatory justice, and group and individual rights.

Social Utility. This point in the affirmative action debate focuses on social outcomes of public policy, or on what is sometimes termed the *common good* (Fullinwider, 1980; Swanson, 1981). Those who favor preferential treatment argue that it enhances the common good by providing better educational and employment opportunities to disadvantaged groups. This in turn helps reduce poverty and unemployment within such groups, thereby providing positive educational and occupational role models for the young, increasing the self-esteem of disadvantaged groups, and reducing government expenditures by breaking the cycle of poverty. The social integration that would accompany expanded opportunities for minority groups would help mitigate negative ethnic, racial, and sexual stereotypes. In addition, as the number of women and racial/ethnic minorities in professions such as law and medicine increased, disadvantaged communities would receive better services. Bok (1985) acknowledges that these goals, taking account of the significant role that parents' education and occupation play in the academic attainment of their offspring, thereby reflect the long view, and that it may take several decades to see results.

Those wary of preferential treatment counter the preceding arguments in several ways. Some note that what constitutes the common good is far from settled. If it is the sum of individuals' good, how is it measured or assessed? Moreover, the meaning of the term *common good* can change, perhaps putting previously favored groups at a disadvantage. If, as Justice Powell asserted in the case of *Regents of the University of California* v. *Bakke* (1978), "the United States is a 'nation of minorities,' then concepts of majority and minority necessarily reflect temporary arrangements and political judgments" (cited in Dreyfuss and Lawrence, 1979, p. 209).

Those skeptical of some affirmative action programs note that the real consequences of policy changes, no matter how well intentioned such changes are, cannot be foreseen. Rather than decreasing racial animosity, preferential treatment may aggravate it by creating resentment among white males and other groups that are not designated as disadvantaged or needy (Beer, 1985; Gibney, 1988; Glazer, 1983; Swanson, 1981). Groups seen as newly favored because of their race or ethnicity may become targets of the majority's animosity, or they may be seen as needing special treatment because of their supposed inferiority. Loury (1987, p. 100) wonders whether "something approximating equality of respect and standing in the eyes of one's fellow citizens" is possible for members of groups regularly reliant on preferential treatment. In the *Bakke* (1978) case, Justice Powell remarked on the "inherent unfairness of, and the perception of mistreatment that accompanies, a system of allocating benefits and privileges on the basis of skin color and ethnic origin" (cited in Swanson, 1981, p. 261).

Those who question the social utility of affirmative action also note the lack of evidence demonstrating that racial/ethnic minorities in such professions as law and medicine actually serve the racial/ethnic minority communities in which such services are not adequately provided by whites (Dreyfuss and Lawrence, 1979; Swanson, 1981).

Distributive Justice. A second point in the philosophical discussion of affirmative action concerns the ways in which various burdens and resources (including, perhaps, jobs and education) are allocated among the citizenry, as well as a government's obligation to ensure that those lowest on the socioeconomic ladder have better opportunities and improved economic status. The crux of the disagreement between those who do and those who do not favor preferential treatment is the basis on which such benefits as status and wealth should be conferred. Should the criteria involve individual abilities and performance (often termed *merit*), or should they involve inherited characteristics, such as race? Opponents of preferential treatment contend that individual merit should determine who gets what, and they may suggest that, in a system that guarantees all citizens certain rights, "likes must be treated alike" (Fullinwider, 1980, p. 13). In other words, race is never an acceptable basis for a decision. Justice Powell expressed this view in the *Bakke* (1978) case by observing, "Racial and ethnic distinctions of *any sort* are suspect" (cited in Dreyfuss and Lawrence, 1979, p. 209), an opinion echoed recently by Justice O'Connor ("Excerpts . . . ," 1989, p. 12). Also disturbing to opponents of preferential treatment is the role that government plays in creating or enforcing programs that differentiate among applicants or candidates on the basis of characteristics other than merit: because the role of government is to remove barriers to equal opportunity—through, for example, laws prohibiting discrimination on the basis of color or sex—it is seen as perverse to put government in the position of, first, requiring employers or institutions to make such distinctions and, second, punishing them by withholding funds when they fail to make the distinctions (Glazer, 1983; Swanson, 1981).

Proponents maintain that preferential treatment is necessary, to give more opportunity to groups long underrepresented in education and employment and reverse the concentration of wealth and power held by white males. Preferential treatment does not require hiring and promoting of the unqualified (those who lack merit), but it does mean expanding the pool of qualified applicants to include members of previously excluded groups. Assuming that pervasive and long-standing racism and sexism in American society have greatly influenced the current distribution of wealth and power, this view allows recognition and consideration of race and gender in admissions and employment decisions, since these characteristics have been the basis of harmful discrimination in the first place.

Race, the proponents of preferential treatment argue, is not an irrelevant physical characteristic (like hair color, for example). Dreyfuss and Lawrence (1979, p. 101) state that the "significance of race is not color but experience"; the kinds of experience shared by members of a given race are likely to bring valuable diversity to academic and work environments. Besides, as one professor (Gillespie, 1988, p. 238) notes about university teaching, "Academic positions in this country have historically been awarded on the basis of race and sex; the race was white and the sex was male."

Those who favor preferential treatment are not troubled by the role that government plays in the policy. They say that because such conditions as slavery, segregation, and denial of civil rights were state-sanctioned, it is appropriate for government to help the affected parties (or their descendants) to reach the levels of wealth, status, and power that they might have reached in the absence of these conditions. Justice Marshall (cited in Greenhouse, 1989a, p. A19) has argued that "a profound difference separates governmental actions that themselves are racist, and governmental actions that seek to remedy the effects of prior racism or to prevent neutral governmental activity from perpetuating the effects of such racism."

Compensatory Justice. This is an idea related to, but more specific and limited than, distributive justice. It involves compensation from the party who has committed an injury to the wronged party (or to that party's descendants). While it is generally accepted that "persons injured by past or ongoing discrimination" (Swanson, 1981, p. 255) are entitled to compensation, disagreement exists about who is owed what and about who should pay.

Those against preferential treatment argue that it penalizes white males who personally have committed no illegal discrimination and who must forgo educational or employment opportunities so that a broad social good, or something approaching justice, can be achieved. The white male is treated as less than equal to the favored party—in essence, he is paying for the wrongs of previous generations.

Advocates of preferential treatment emphasize the importance of remedying the effects of society's past and current discrimination, which has prevented many from reaching what Justice Marshall (cited in Swanson, 1981, p. 163) calls "meaningful equality." Preferential policies may temporarily discriminate against some white males, the advocates say, but public policy decisions always harm some interests (Fullinwider, 1980; Swanson, 1981). Krauthammer (1985, p. 10) summarizes the arguments about compensatory justice by noting the difficulty of settling claims of "a historically oppressed community for redress, and of the blameless individual for equal treatment."

Group and Individual Rights. This point concerns the following question: Granted that discrimination exists, should society (or government) assume that all members of a particular group have been affected by it in the same way and are therefore entitled to preferential treatment? Traditionally, American justice has held that rights belong to individual persons: the individual is seen as the "ultimate entity" (Morris, 1986, p. 1211), and color-blindness, or refusal to base decisions on race, ethnic origin, or sex is seen as the proper policy. Those who are wary of preferential treatment maintain this view and argue that only those individuals who can demonstrate that they have been discriminated against are entitled to special treatment. Further, they suggest that providing special treatment on the basis of group membership is not likely to help those most injured by discrimination (Beer, 1985); "it will favor the young instead of the old, the trained over the untrained" (Fullinwider, 1980, p. 66).

Defenders of affirmative action assert that preferential treatment on the basis of group membership is at least temporarily permissible, in order "to remedy the effects of past discrimination against historically disadvantaged groups" (Swanson, 1981, p. 260). As the dissenting justices observed in the Bakke (1978) case, being a member of a "general class of persons likely to have been the victims of discrimination" is justification enough for preferential treatment (cited in Swanson, 1981, p. 262).

Considerations for the Student Affairs Administrator

Fullinwider (1980, p. 8) believes that "there are not many decisive answers to be found in the [affirmative action] controversy." This assessment recognizes the hard fact that fundamental differences sometimes separate proponents and opponents of preferential treatment. While some of the issues may seem more appropriate to the ivory tower than to the administrative office, they are related to practical decisions of affirmative action implementation. To serve as effective agents of affirmative action on campus, whatever its form may be, administrators need to have a working knowledge of the philosophical arguments discussed here, and they must consider and define their own views and positions.

As an exercise for student affairs administrators and their staffs, we suggest a two-hour meeting to discuss the following four questions:

1. Is it permissible or desirable to favor some applicants or employees because of their minority status?
2. How much effort should the university make to recruit and retain minority students and employees? What form should such effort take?
3. What does the university value in a student body: academic performance and potential (as measured by grades and test scores), or other, noncognitive characteristics, such as multicultural experience?
4. How is the merit of employees measured?

It may be wise to distribute these questions to the staff a week before the meeting, and to develop brief hypothetical vignettes that bring the questions alive. Staff members will probably represent various views and positions, and it is important for administrators to understand the philosophical roots of the affirmative action debate before moderating or facilitating discussions.

Student affairs staff and students themselves often have strong feelings for or against preferential treatment (see Ponterotto, Martinez, and Hayden, 1986), yet few campus personnel feel free to express their true views. The goal of this exercise is to provide a supportive environment where strong feelings are allowed to emerge. Once the debate is open and on the table, constructive discussion (and, it is hoped, consensus) can emerge with respect to future affirmative action efforts.

An important first step in creating an organized, staff-supported affirmative action program is to understand the program's history, definition, and rationale. Equally important, however, is an understanding of the legal basis of affirmative action. Being comfortable with one's position on affirmative action is important, but one must also ask, "Is my position consistent with the intent of civil rights law and with its interpretation by the Supreme Court?" How, for example, has the court specifically interpreted "appropriate" affirmative action? What is the court's stand on the color-blind–race-conscious debate? What is the court's view of race-based quotas and other affirmative action–designed mechanisms? Chapter Three presents an up-to-date and comprehensive treatment of the legal side of affirmative action.

References

Beer, W. R. "View from the Trenches: Affirmative Action in Brooklyn." *New Republic,* Jan. 18, 1985, pp. 17–19.

Bok, D. "Admitting Success: The Case for Racial Preferences." *New Republic,* Feb. 4, 1985, pp. 14–16.

Brimelow, P. "U.S. Apartheid? Race Discrimination Is Seeping Back into the Civil-Rights Laws." *Barron's,* Aug. 25, 1986, p. 11.

Dreyfuss, J. D., and Lawrence, C. *The Bakke Case: The Politics of Inequality.* San Diego, Calif.: Harcourt Brace Jovanovich, 1979.

"Excerpts from Court Opinions in Voiding of Richmond's Contracting Plan." *New York Times,* Jan. 24, 1989, p. 12.

Fullinwider, R. K. *The Reverse Discrimination Controversy: A Moral and Legal Analysis.* Totowa, N.J.: Rowman and Allenheld, 1980.

Gibney, J. S. "The Berkeley Squeeze: The Future of Affirmative Action." *New Republic,* Apr. 11, 1988, pp. 15–17.

Gillespie, P. "Campus Stories, or the Cat Beyond the Canvas." *Vital Speeches of the Day,* 1988, 54 (8), 235–238.

Glazer, N. *Ethnic Dilemmas, 1964–1982.* Cambridge, Mass.: Harvard University Press, 1983.

Greenhouse, L. "Court Bars a Plan Set Up to Provide Jobs to Minorities." *New York Times,* Jan. 24, 1989a, pp. A1, A19.

Greenhouse, L. "Signal on Job Rights." *New York Times,* Jan. 25, 1989b, pp. A1, A18.

Hofstadter, R. *The American Political Tradition.* New York: Knopf, 1977.

Krauthammer, C. "A Defense of Quotas." *New Republic,* Sept. 16, 1985, pp. 9–11.

Loury, G. C. "Why Preferential Admission Is Not Enough for Blacks." *Chronicle of Higher Education,* Mar. 25, 1987, p. 100.

Mann, M. E. "The Department of Justice and Affirmative Action." *Journal of Intergroup Relations,* 1987, *15* (1), 5–10.

Morris, A. A. "Affirmative Action and 'Quota' Systems." *Education Law Reporter,* 1986, *28,* 1203–1235.

Ponterotto, J. G., Martinez, F. M., and Hayden, D. C. "Student Affirmative Action Programs: A Help or Hindrance to Minority Graduate Students?" *Journal of College Student Personnel,* 1986, *27* (4), 318–325.

Salomone, R. C. *Equal Education Under Law: Legal Rights and Federal Policy in the Post-Brown Era.* New York: St. Martin's, 1986.

Sowell, T. "*Weber* and *Bakke,* and the Presuppositions of Affirmative Action." *Wayne Law Review,* 1980, *26* (4), 1309–1336.

Swanson, K. *Affirmative Action and Preferential Admissions in Higher Education: An Annotated Bibliography.* Metuchen, N.J.: Scarecrow Press, 1981.

"True Affirmative Action: Who's Kidding Whom About Goals and Quotas?" *New Republic,* Sept. 16, 1985, pp. 4, 49.

Weiss, R. J. "Affirmative Action: A Brief History." *Journal of Intergroup Relations,* 1987, *15* (2), 40–53.

Cases Cited

Regents of the University of California v. *Bakke,* 438 U.S. 265 (1978).

Robin Bullington is a doctoral student in counseling psychology at the University of Houston.

Joseph G. Ponterotto is associate professor of counseling and counseling psychology in the Division of Psychological and Educational Services, Graduate School of Education, Fordham University–Lincoln Center, New York.

Student affairs administrators should have a basic understanding of legal issues as they apply to affirmative action policy.

Legal Aspects of Affirmative Action

Diane E. Lewis, Lindsay J. Lewis, Joseph G. Ponterotto

"An individual's view of affirmative action is shaped by his or her moral and political beliefs, by his or her own vision of society and justice" (Lamber, 1987, p. 247). How the student affairs administrator introduces and emphasizes affirmative action policies in his or her department and throughout the campus is largely a matter of institutional and personal philosophy. Nevertheless, there are certain legal guidelines that the student affairs administrator must understand and follow. Although the administrator cannot be expected to have legal expertise in affirmative action, he or she should have a basic grounding in the legal mandates and consequences surrounding affirmative action policy. The goal of this chapter is to present a comprehensive overview of affirmative action from the legal perspective.

Specifically, this chapter examines constitutional and statutory rights and the most significant judicial interpretations of civil rights law that affect affirmative action on campus. The reader interested in an expanded treatment of legal issues in student services is referred to Barr (1983, 1988) generally and to Seaquist (1988) specifically.

Civil Rights Laws

This section reviews the civil rights laws most relevant to affirmative action issues. Briefly covered are the Fifth and Fourteenth Amendments, Section 1981 of the Civil Rights Act of 1866, Section 1983 of the Civil Rights Act of 1871, Title VI and Title VII of the Civil Rights Act of 1964, Title IX of the Education Amendments of 1972, Section 504 of the Rehabilitation Act of 1973, and the Age Discrimination Act of 1975.

Federal Constitutional Provisions. The Fourteenth Amendment is the most frequently cited federal constitutional provision in cases involving discrimination and affirmation action. Adopted shortly after the Civil War, the amendment is aimed at prohibiting certain discriminatory conduct by state governments. Section 1 of the Fourteenth Amendment provides in relevant part that "no State shall . . . deny to any person within its jurisdiction the equal protection of the laws." Although the guarantee of equal protection is not expressly applicable to the federal government, subsequent court decisions have interpreted the Fifth Amendment to impose on the federal government the same equal-protection obligations imposed on states by the Fourteenth Amendment.

These constitutional amendments apply to all state universities and colleges but not to most private educational institutions. Where a private party is closely connected with the state, its conduct may be deemed to be equivalent to governmental action, or "state action," as it is described by the courts. In this relatively rare circumstance, the federal constitutional provision can be applied to a private university. Before subjecting a private institution to this constitutional standard, courts have required a greater connection than mere receipt of federal funds.

Section 1981 of the Civil Rights Act of 1866 (42 U.S.C. sec. 1981). Section 1981 provides that racial minorities have the same rights as white citizens to "make and enforce contracts" (42 U.S.C. sec. 1981). Section 1981 is based on the Thirteenth Amendment (prohibition of slavery) and applies to both the public and the private sector. The statute prohibits discrimination against racial minorities in school admissions and in hiring decisions, but it does not cover discriminatory acts after the initial contract is made (see *Patterson* v. *McLean Credit Union*, 1989).

To comply with Section 1981, the administrator must be sure that racial/ethnic minority students and staff have the same benefits and privileges as their white counterparts. Promises made in catalogues, brochures, and other literature must apply equally to white and nonwhite students and staff. Since universities routinely enter into contractual agreements with students and staff (for example, with respect to housing, parking, and food-service contracts), there is a significant potential for lawsuits to be brought under Section 1981 (Seaquist, 1988).

To prevail in a Section 1981 case, the plaintiff must introduce prima facie proof of discriminatory intent. Given the difficulties of proving purposeful discrimination, relatively few higher education cases are brought under this provision (Seaquist, 1988). A successful plaintiff in a Section 1981 case may receive a monetary award as compensation and, in some circumstances, a court-ordered injunction to remedy the violation (Cox, 1988). When the defendant's conduct has been egregious, the plaintiff may receive punitive damages, an extra monetary award intended solely as punishment of the defendant.

Section 1983 of the Civil Rights Act of 1871 (42 U.S.C. sec. 1983). To establish a claim under Section 1983, a plaintiff must prove, first, that he or she has been denied a right protected either by the Constitution or by federal law and, second, that the defendant was acting "under color of state law" (Seaquist, 1988). Acting "under color of state law" is essentially the same as the "state action" concept already mentioned, and it implies a close connection between the defendant and the state or federal government. A state university is deemed to act "under color of state law," but a private university or college generally is not. The defendant in a Section 1983 lawsuit must "have exercised power 'possessed by virtue of state law and made possible only because the wrongdoer is clothed with the authority of state law'" (*West* v. *Atkins*, 1988, p. 49). (The reader is referred to Seaquist, 1988, for a detailed discussion of this topic.)

If a plaintiff can prove that his or her constitutional or federal rights have been violated and that the defendant is connected to the government, then he or she may be awarded compensatory damages, punitive damages, and equitable relief (Cox, 1988). Further, if the court should find for the plaintiff, then the state or federal government may insist that the college or university comply with Section 1983.

Title VI of the Civil Rights Act of 1964 (42 U.S.C. sec. 2000d et seq.). Title VI prohibits public and private institutions that receive federal funds from discriminating on the basis of race, color, or national origin. Title VI does not apply to discrimination based on sex or religion. Practices having a disparate effect, whether intentional or not, on members of a protected class are defined as discriminatory.

Race, color, and national origin may be taken into account in attempts to diversity the student population, and race may also be used as a factor in attempts to mitigate the effects of past discrimination. Title VI prohibits a college or a university from using race as the sole factor in a candidate's selection for admission, hiring, or promotion. (The broad language in Title VI is interpreted and implemented by Department of Education regulations; the interested reader should begin with Seaquist, 1988.)

If racial discrimination is found in a program that receives federal financial assistance, the Department of Education may make an informal attempt to achieve Title VI compliance. If this approach is unsuccessful, then federal funding can be withdrawn after a notice, a hearing, and federal review. The Department of Education may also recommend action by the Justice Department.

Title VII of the Civil Rights Act of 1964 (42 U.S.C. sec. 2000 et seq.). Title VII applies only to employment and prohibits job-related discrimination on the basis of race, color, sex, religion, or national origin. Title VII mandates fair practices in hiring, training, supervision, and termination. To be equitable, employment practices must follow the procedures of the personnel department and be applied consistently throughout the campus.

With respect to Title VII, student affairs administrators should be knowledgeable about personnel interviewing. For example, photographs should not be requested of applicants, and the candidate should not be asked during an interview about his or her age, marital status, family situation, religion, or ethnic background. Educational background should be discussed only if it is relevant to the position. Jobs should be posted and advertised in places where any interested party can see the listing, and job qualifications should reflect the skills that are strictly necessary.

Title VII also encompasses on-the-job situations that are considered discriminatory. Any staff member involved in personnel issues should be familiar with these situations. In general, language differences and differences in religious observances must be tolerated. Absences due to pregnancy must be allowed insofar as disability and sick-leave benefits apply, and a job must be guaranteed after pregnancy leave if positions are guaranteed for employees returning from disability leave (see Pregnancy Discrimination Act, 42 U.S.C. sec. 2000e-2, 1978).

Sexual harassment is defined under Title VII as unwelcome sexual advances, requests for sexual favors, and other verbal or physical conduct of a sexual nature when connected to employment. Administrators should note that the employer is liable for the actions of employees, whether or not the employer is aware of employees' actions.

Under Title VII, the reasons for termination of employment should be well documented, as well as clearly and exclusively related to job performance. Existing personnel policies must be followed to the letter.

Title IX of the Education Amendments of 1972 (20 U.S.C. secs. 1681-1686). Title IX prohibits discrimination on the basis of sex in any educational institution receiving federal financial assistance. Some organizations and activities are exempt from the application of Title IX, including schools run by religious organizations, by the military, or by the merchant marine; social fraternities and voluntary youth-service organizations; certain youth conferences; father-son and mother-daughter days; and scholarship awards in so-called beauty pageants. Furthermore, Title IX expressly permits private undergraduate institutions to be single-sex schools.

Title IX is directly connected to the practice of student affairs administration, in several relevant ways. In *admissions*, gender may not be used preferentially except in private, single-sex undergraduate schools. During any interview for admissions, hiring, or promotion, questions related to the candidate's marital or family status are not permitted. Campus *housing* and other facilities may be segregated by sex, but the segregated facilities must be comparable. *Courses* must be offered to all students. *Sports* teams may be separate, but both sexes must have equal access to athletic supplies and finances; if this is not possible, then all students must be allowed to try out for all teams, with the exception of contact sports. *Counseling* and *employ-*

ment assistance must apply equally to both sexes. Two issues are of particular interest here. First, when a school offers employment opportunities outside the school (for example, through job listings and cooperative education internships), these opportunities must be offered on a nondiscriminatory basis. Second, counselors should avoid sex-based stereotypes in advising students on career decisions. Where full *health care* is offered to students, gynecological care must be included. A leave of absence must be granted for conditions related to pregnancy and childbirth insofar as disability and sick-leave benefits apply. (The reader is referred to Seaquist, 1988, for a deeper discussion of the regulations implementing Title IX.)

Title IX prohibits discrimination even when the educational institution receives federal funding indirectly, such as through federal student assistance programs (see *Grove City College* v. *Bell,* 1984, p. 569-570, and the discussion by Seaquist, 1988). The Supreme Court in the *Grove City College* case interpreted Title IX as applying only to the specific educational program or activity receiving federal funding, but this ruling was changed by legislation when Congress enacted the Civil Rights Restoration Act of 1987, to make clear that Title IX applies to all the operations of a college or a university that receives federal funding, and not just to specific programs. The student affairs administrator must understand the provisions of Title IX and know when and where federal funding is being used to pay for programs.

Section 504 of the Rehabilitation Act of 1973 (29 U.S.C. secs. 791-794). Section 504 provides protection to handicapped individuals in any college or university program that receives direct or indirect federal funds. A *handicapped person* is defined as one who "has a physical or mental impairment which substantially limits one or more major life activities," who "has a record of such an impairment," or who "is regarded as having such an impairment."

Because understanding which impairments qualify as handicaps can be confusing, Section 504 should be studied. Section 504 requires that housing, classrooms, and services be accessible. Admissions examinations must be administered so that a handicapped candidate can take them with an equal chance of success. All courses must be available to the student if he or she could succeed safely, even if adaptations in equipment and scheduling become necessary. Counseling services must be equivalent, especially in the career area, and financial aid must be equitable.

The Age Discrimination Act of 1975 (42 U.S.C. sec. 6101 et seq.). The Age Discrimination Act prohibits age-based discrimination in federally funded programs and activities, in public as well as private colleges and universities. This law is relevant to every student affairs program supported by federal funds, ranging from admissions to employment. Unless there are certain ages at which a person could not be expected to succeed safely in a given area, age discrimination is prohibited.

Supreme Court Decisions

With this basic understanding of the relevant civil rights laws, we can now proceed to a discussion of recent court actions. The Supreme Court has decided more than a dozen affirmative action cases since the *Regents of the University of California* v. *Bakke* (1978) "reverse discrimination" case brought this issue into sharp focus more than a decade ago. These cases have tended to divide the court; in some instances, the differences have prevented the justices from issuing opinions endorsed by the majority of the court. Three major affirmative action cases in the 1985 term alone produced fourteen separate opinions. Lamber (1987, p. 247) suggests that this discord in the Supreme Court's opinions "parallels political divisions, public disagreements as well as theoretical uncertainties," encompassed by our society as a whole. Table 1 presents a summary of the principal affirmative action and discrimination cases decided since the *Bakke* case.

Our objective in the following section is to analyze relevant decisions, from the *Bakke* case through the Supreme Court's 1988 term. Although these rulings have not been models of clarity, they have resolved certain issues and provided guidance about permissible and impermissible conduct in both the public and the private sector.

It is important for student affairs administrators to understand how Supreme Court affirmative action decisions affect their institutions. This section briefly examines issues that have been emerging from recent affirmative action cases: the current status of the "race-conscious–color-blind" debate; affirmative action from a private and a public institutional perspective; the legitimacy of using quotas to enhance pluralism on campus; the relevance of statistical imbalance in proving discrimination; analysis of disparate treatment and disparate impact; and the legitimacy of using layoffs and consent decrees in attempts to create a more equitable racial/gender distribution on campus.

Trends in the "Race-Conscious–Color-Blind" Debate. Until the Supreme Court's recent decision in *City of Richmond* v. *J. A. Croson Co.* (1989), there was no consensus on whether race-conscious remedial measures would be judged by the same rigorous standards as legislation that tended to discriminate against racial/ethnic minorities. Several of the justices had suggested, in previous rulings, that remedial or "benign" measures should be reviewed under a less stringent standard, although this view was never shared by the majority. In *Croson*, six justices voted that any legislative classifications based on race, even if the law involves a remedial affirmative action program, must satisfy the "strict scrutiny" test. As the term implies, *strict scrutiny* invites "searching judicial inquiry into the justification for such race-based measures, . . . to 'smoke out' illegitimate uses of race" (p. 4139). Although affirmative action is still a permissible goal under the Fourteenth Amendment, the court's decision requires that the program be

Table 1. Supreme Court Affirmative Action and Selected Civil Rights Cases, 1978–1989

Case	Defendant(s)	Issue	Basis of Challenge	Decision	Vote
Price Waterhouse v. Hopkins (1989)	Private employer	Refusal to hire or promote (gender)	Title VII	Employer has burden of proving nondiscrimination	6–3
Wards Cove Packing Company, Inc. v. Atonio (1989)	Private employer	Who has burden of proof in disparate-impact case?	Title VII	Employee has burden of proof; procedures and statistical comparisons established	5–4
Martin v. Wilks (1989)	Public employer	May an affirmative action plan entered by a consent decree be challenged by employees who were not parties to the original lawsuit?	Title VII	Consent decree may be challenged	5–4
Patterson v. McLean Credit Union (1989)	Private employer	On-the-job racial harassment	Sec. 1981	Sec. 1981 does not apply	5–4
City of Richmond v. J. A. Croson Company (1989)	Municipality	Set-aside of funds for minority contracting firms	Constitution: equal protection	Set-aside impermissible	6–3
Watson v. Fort Worth Bank & Trust (1988)	Private employer (bank)	Disparate impact of subjective hiring and promotion criteria	Title VII	Remanded back to district court; disparate impact may be used	—
Johnson v. Santa Clara County Transportation Agency (1987)	Public employer (county transportation agency)	Voluntary plan to promote women	Title VII	Program permissible	6–3

Table 1. (*continued*)

Case	Defendant(s)	Issue	Basis of Challenge	Decision	Vote
United States v. Paradise (1987)	Public employer (state department of public safety)	Court-ordered promotions quota for blacks	Constitution: equal protection	Quota permissible	5-4
Local #93, International Association of Firefighters, AFL–CIO v. City of Cleveland (1986)	Public employer (city fire department)	Consent decree providing for promotion quota for blacks	Title VII	Quota permissible	6-3
Local #28 of the Sheet Metal Workers' International Association v. Equal Employment Opportunity Commission (1986)	Labor union	Court-ordered quota for admitting blacks to union	Title VII; Constitution; equal protection, due-process guarantee	Quota permissible	5-4
Wygant v. Jackson Board of Education (1986)	Public employer (school board)	Voluntary agreement to modify seniority rule for layoffs to preserve jobs for blacks	Constitution: equal protection	Layoffs not permissible	5-4
Firefighters Local Union #1784 v. Stotts (1980)	Public employer (city fire department)	Court order overriding seniority rights in layoffs to protect recently hired blacks	Title VII	Order not permissible	6-3
Fullilove v. Klutznick (1980)	Congress and secretary of commerce	10 percent federal funding set-aside for minority-firm contracts	Constitution: equal protection, due-process guarantee	Set-aside permissible	6-3
United Steelworkers of America v. Weber (1979)	Labor union and private employer	Voluntary quota for blacks in training program	Title VII	Quota permissible	5-2
Regents of the University of California v. Bakke (1978)	State medical school	Voluntary admissions quota for blacks	Title VI; Constitution: equal protection	Quota impermissible; some race considerations permissible	5-4

"narrowly tailored" to remedy "identified discrimination" (p. 4142). These requirements do not mandate a completely color-blind approach, but they do impose significant restrictions in adopting race-conscious remedies on state and local governments.

The *Croson* decision represents a change in the direction of affirmative action jurisprudence. With the arrival of Justices Scalia and Kennedy on the court, a new coalition has resolved the long-standing issues about the applicability of strict scrutiny. During the 1985 term, the Supreme Court appeared to be moving slowly and cautiously toward allowing certain race-conscious affirmative action programs under Title VII and the Fourteenth Amendment (Clague, 1987). The rationale for such programs was the desire to eradicate current discrimination and the effects of past discrimination. The significance of the court's adoption of strict scrutiny for affirmative action programs is difficult to overstate. One commentator has observed that "as equal protection law has developed over the last several decades, a statute that is subjected to 'strict scrutiny' analysis almost never survives such scrutiny" (Greenhouse, 1989a, p. A19). Just as the Court's previous affirmative action record seems to parallel society's ambivalence on the subject, Justice Marshall commented in his dissenting opinion in *Croson* that "a majority of this Court signals that it regards racial discrimination as largely a phenomenon of the past, and that government bodies need no longer preoccupy themselves with rectifying racial injustice" (*Croson*, 1989, p. 4155).

The *Croson* court struck down the City of Richmond's affirmative action plan, which set aside 30 percent of public-works funds for contracts with racial/ethnic minority–owned construction companies. The court specifically criticized the Richmond plan because it was not based on evidence of the city's own past discrimination in awarding contracts. Instead, the plan was tied to remedying the effects of past discrimination in the construction industry generally. According to the *Croson* decision, the concept of "societal discrimination" is not sufficient to justify such a plan in the public sector. Richmond's 30 percent set-aside was not tied to the number of qualified racial/ethnic minority contractors available, was not "narrowly tailored" to the relevant need and population, and was seen as a rigid racial quota. The court also criticized the Richmond plan because, contrary to the federal set-asides approved in *Fullilove v. Klutznick* (1980) and *United States v. Paradise* (1987), race-neutral remedies had not been attempted before application of the set-aside.

While the *Croson* decision does not affect the federal racial/ethnic minority–contracting program, it sets a rigorous standard of review for the public sector's affirmative action programs. As highlighted recently in Greenhouse (1989b, p. A18), "By definition, the strict-scrutiny standard is now the starting point for analysis of all such preferences. . . . That description would seem to limit the use of racial preferences to the elimination of patently obvious, egregious discrimination that can be linked to the deliberate acts of identifiable parties. But it is likely that some of the more oblique forms of affirmative action, such as extensive recruiting of minorities, or programs that offer special training, could also survive strict scrutiny because white applicants would have a difficult time persuading courts that their own right to constitutional equal protection had been violated by programs that emphasize inclusion of all rather than exclusion [at] the expense of some."

Public Versus Private Institutions. The laws that apply to affirmative action issues vary with the type of educational institution involved. The *Croson* case and the Supreme Court's other rulings on the Fourteenth Amendment apply only to state universities and colleges, as well as to a few private universities whose close connections with the state elevate their conduct to the level of "state action." Similarly, the provisions of Section 1983 are limited to regulating public institutions and these few private universities. Any affirmative action program implemented by one of these institutions will be judged by the "strict scrutiny" standard. The implications for affirmative action programs in state universities are not specifically addressed, although it is clear that proposed remedial measures must minimize any "benign" discrimination against whites. Programs that benefit racial/ethnic minorities by excluding others on the basis of race must be narrowly drawn to meet an identified inequity. In general, the greater the exclusion, the greater the burden of justifying the proposed remedy.

The legality of an affirmative action program at a private institution is tested by federal legislation and not by the Constitution. Section 1981 prohibits discrimination in school admissions and hiring, and Title VII prohibits employment-related discrimination. Title VI, Title IX, and the Rehabilitation Act legislate against discrimination at any college or university that receives direct or indirect federal funding. These statutes may provide a basis for broader remedial measures than are permitted by the Fourteenth Amendment. The *Croson* court expressly recognized that the United States Congress is empowered by the Fourteenth Amendment to enact remedial legislation otherwise prohibited by the Constitution (*City of Richmond v. J. A. Croson Co.*, 1989, p. 4142). There is no clear answer to the question of whether this federal legislation will be interpreted as reaching beyond the limitations of the Fourteenth Amendment. Prior rulings have suggested that this legislation should be interpreted the same as the Fourteenth Amendment, or even more restrictively. (In the *Bakke* case, four justices expressed the view that Title VI is "color-blind," and that *no* affirmative action is permitted.)

Whether the university is public or private, the court has recognized the policy-based reasons for allowing greater discretion to educational institutions (see Sexton, 1979). The *Bakke* court, for example, recognized that diverse racial composition of the student body may promote valid goals and policies in an educational institution. In general, undergraduate institutions are given greater justification for preferential treatment to racial/ethnic minorities, in order to achieve diversity, than graduate and professional schools are. Additional considerations come into play in reviewing the policies of sectarian institutions, since the right to free exercise of religion, guaranteed by the First Amendment, must be weighed in assessing the validity of these institutions' conduct.

Quotas. The Supreme Court has consistently criticized the use of quotas in achieving affirmative action goals. In the *Bakke* case, the court invalidated an admissions quota that reserved for disadvantaged racial/ethnic minority students sixteen of the one hundred positions at a medical school. The desire to remedy past discrimination was deemed insufficient justification for a program that excludes white candidates because of their race. While institutional discrimination need not be proved, the intent of such a program must be to diversify the particular student body or work force. As already mentioned, the *Croson* court invalidated a racial/ethnic minority-contracting set-aside as a "rigid quota" unsupported by any adequate justification.

Admissions quotas at a public or a private university are an inappropriate affirmative action remedy, except as a last resort to address *persistent* discrimination *at a specific institution*. The institution would also have to prove that there were no other, less intrusive, alternatives for remedying the situation.

Student affairs administrators should note, however, that racial/ethnic minority status may still be used as one of a number of factors to be considered in attempting to diversify the student body. Recruitment and other creative programs may be used in efforts to increase the number of minority students earning advanced degrees. Flexible goals for racial/ethnic minority recruitment and retention should be permissible in public and private institutions (Clague, 1987). In a public institution, any such program may have to be justified under the "strict scrutiny" test, if challenged.

Statistical Imbalance: Title VII and the Fourteenth Amendment. In *United Steelworkers of America* v. *Weber* (1979) the Supreme Court found that Title VII does not prohibit preferential hiring and training of racial/ethnic minority candidates, if the employer seeks to remedy a "manifest . . . imbalance in traditionally segregated job categories" (p. 197). In the *Weber* case, a white employee challenged a voluntary affirmative action program, which held half the places in a craft-training program at the Kaiser Aluminum Corporation open for blacks until the percentage of skilled black craft workers in the plant reflected the percentage of blacks in the labor force. As one commentator has observed, "Justice Brennan practically conceded that Weber's claim was supported by a literal reading of Title VII. But, he broadly concluded, Weber's claim was contrary to the spirit and especially the purpose of the Act, which was revealed by its legislative history" (Morris, 1986, p. 1210). In his opinion in the case,

Justice Brennan noted (p. 490) that it would be "ironic indeed if a law triggered by a Nation's concern over centuries of racial injustice and intended to improve the lot of those who had been 'excluded from the American dream so long' [a reference to the words of Senator Hubert Humphrey] . . . constituted the first legislative prohibition of all voluntary, private, race-conscious efforts to abolish patterns of racial segregation and hierarchy."

Johnson v. *Santa Clara County Transportation Agency* (1987) extended the *Weber* decision into the public sector. The Supreme Court (p. 631 [5a]; p. 632 [5b]) upheld a public employer's right to have a voluntary affirmative action program for women that was based on a statistical imbalance, rather than on specific or direct proof of discrimination: "We do not regard as identical the constraints of Title VII and the federal constitution on voluntarily adopted affirmative action plans. . . . In some cases . . . the manifest imbalance may be sufficiently egregious to establish a prima facie case. However, as long as there is a manifest imbalance, an employer may adopt a plan even where the disparity is not so striking, without being required to introduce the non-statistical evidence of past discrimination that would be demanded by the 'prima facie' standard."

A college or a university considering a voluntary affirmative action plan should note that the court in this case particularly liked the Santa Clara County Transportation Agency's plan because gender and race could be treated as a limited advantage in hiring and promotion in traditionally segregated areas, but a woman or other minority person would have to compete with all other qualified applicants for the position. The court reaffirmed its stand that affirmative action programs are a *temporary* means of rectifying the effects of discrimination and stressed that gender and racial/ethnic minority balance cannot be *maintained* through affirmative action.

These cases imply that, under Title VII, a public or private college may voluntarily engage in preferential hiring or admissions that favor historically oppressed minorities, to correct statistical imbalances *in its own work force or student body,* as compared with the *relevant pool of applicants.* A public or private university may initiate voluntary programs that attempt to increase minority representation among faculty and students through recruitment efforts and through programs that try to increase the number of minority students earning various degrees. It is highly likely that even an institution without a demonstrated history of discrimination may take specific steps (such as establishing goals for recruitment and retention) to increase minority representation in the faculty and in the student body, on the basis of statistical imbalance (Clague, 1987).

Disparate Treatment in a Title VII Case. Under Title VII, considerations of "sex, race, religion, and nation of origin are not relevant to the selection, evaluation, or compensation of employees" (*Price Waterhouse* v. *Hopkins,* 1989, p. 4472). In the employment context, discrimination may be shown by direct evidence of discriminatory intent or by indirect statistical proofs that link an employment practice with a discriminatory outcome. Proof of discriminatory intent, or "disparate treatment," can be difficult to establish when employers wish to disguise their motives. In many circumstances, statistical evidence of "disparate impact" may be the only practical method of proof for the plaintiff.

In *Price Waterhouse* v. *Hopkins,* the Supreme Court addressed the burdens of proof in a Title VII disparate-treatment case. The plaintiff in the *Hopkins* case alleged that her employer failed to promote her because of gender stereotypes. The employer disputed her evidence of discriminatory treatment by arguing that it had a legitimate nondiscriminatory reason for not offering the promotion to the plaintiff. Where permissible and illegitimate motivations are simultaneously present, it is the employer's obligation, in a disparate-treatment case, to prove that it acted properly. The employer must carry its burden by a preponderance of the evidence or, in other words, it must prove that its legitimate motives are more likely than not to be the reason why the plaintiff was not promoted.

Although the Supreme Court's decision in the *Hopkins* case addressed gender discrimination as a reason for failing to give promotions, the court's reasoning is equally applicable to racial discrimination, or to discrimination in other employment contexts, but its application is limited because actual discriminatory intent is often difficult to prove. Different considerations apply to cases that are based on statistical proof of disparate impact.

Disparate Impact in a Title VII Case. In contrast with the requirement for proof of actual discriminatory motives under the disparate-treatment test, a plaintiff may use statistical proof for support under the disparate-impact theory. In unintentional employment discrimination (that is, practices discriminatory in effect but not in intent), or in intentional cases where a discriminatory motive is hard to prove, "a plaintiff may prove a Title VII violation by showing that the employment practice in question has an improper disparate impact according to race or sex" (Adelman, 1987, p. 407).

In *Watson* v. *Fort Worth Bank & Trust* (1988), the disparate-impact analysis was interpreted as including such subjective evaluation criteria as interviews, rating scales, and experience requirements, as well as such objective criteria as standardized tests. (For a discussion of disparate-treatment and disparate-impact analysis and the *Watson* case, the reader is referred to Adelman, 1987, and Bersoff, 1988.)

In *Wards Cove Packing Company, Inc.* v. *Atonio* (1989), a bare five-member majority redefined the burdens on a plaintiff in a Title VII lawsuit brought under disparate-impact theory. An employer may use business justifications to support an employment practice that has a discriminatory effect. In a shift from previous precedent (see Bales, 1989b, and the *Watson* case), the court placed "the ultimate burden of proving that discrimination against a protected group has been caused by a specific employment practice [on] the plaintiff at all times" (*Watson v. Fort Worth Bank & Trust,* 1988, p. 4927). In responding to an employer's business justifications, the plaintiff must also demonstrate that nondiscriminatory alternatives are available. These alternatives must be as effective as the employer's existing practices in achieving legitimate nondiscriminatory goals (see the *Wards Cove* case, p. 4588). According to Wayne Camara, director of scientific affairs at the American Psychological Association's Scientific Directorate (cited in Bales, 1989a, p. 7), "This sets a major precedent for cases dealing with adverse impact. . . . The balance of power, I think, has shifted dramatically to the employer."

Also noteworthy in the *Wards Cove* case is the majority's definitive statement that in cases where statistical evidence is important, the relevant statistical comparison is the racial composition of employees hired in a given position or field with respect to the relevant labor force.

The practical implications of these cases are that public and private universities must clearly understand what they are looking at when they evaluate candidates, faculty, students, and staff. Subjective measures must be handled carefully. Interviewers need to know what qualities and qualifications they are looking for, and they must be able to support their judgments. Such caution will enable the institution to avoid unintentional discrimination and Title VII suits. It also gives schools the opportunity to weigh some nontraditional abilities and experiences in a way that could give advantages to the unique experiences of racial/ethnic minority and women candidates (Lawrence, 1988; see also Atkinson, Staso, and Hosford, 1978; Tracey and Sedlacek, 1985).

Layoffs. There is no Supreme Court precedent for affirmative action–based layoffs under Title VII or the Fourteenth Amendment (see *Firefighters Local Union #1784 v. Stotts,* 1980, and *Wygant v. Jackson Board of Education,* 1986). The court has repeatedly voiced its concern that, as Justice Brennan said in the *Weber* case (1979, p. 492), affirmative action layoff plans "unnecessarily trammel the interests of white employees."

Not all affirmative action–based layoff plans have been precluded under Title VII or the Fourteenth Amendment. Nevertheless, it is highly unlikely that any college or university trying to justify the use of a special layoff plan to protect untenured minorities (during retrenchment, for example) would succeed (Clague, 1987). A college or a university could consider offering early- and partial-retirement programs and incentives as an alternative (Clague, 1987). This practice would create new openings and would lessen the impact of retrenchment on racial/ethnic minorities and women, who are usually the most recently hired and therefore the first to be let go.

Consent Decrees. As an effect of the 1985 Supreme Court term, consent decrees may be used in both the public and the private sector to achieve affirmative action goals. Public and private institutions of higher education may negotiate race-conscious settlements to Title VII suits, without admitting to a history of discrimination. While a court cannot order affirmative action–based hiring and promotion, except on the basis of a constitutional violation, a public or private college or university may agree to such a plan voluntarily. Since a proved history of discrimination is not required in reaching these settlements, affected students or employees do not have to be actual victims of discrimination (Clague, 1987).

The recent Supreme Court decision in *Martin v. Wilks* (1989) has undermined the long-term benefits of consent decrees. In this case, a consent decree was challenged by a group of white employees, who claimed that the plan made them victims of "reverse discrimination." By a bare five-member majority, the court ruled that affected individuals who have not been parties to an earlier job-discrimination lawsuit may challenge an affirmative action plan mandated by a consent decree.

A challenge to an established consent decree will still have to win its case on its own merits (see *Martin v. Wilks,* 1989, for a discussion), and a well-conceived and well-supported consent decree will not necessarily be invalid. The court's decision in *Martin v. Wilks* makes it more likely now that an affirmative action plan negotiated by a consent decree will be challenged on grounds of "reverse discrimination," in violation of Title VII.

Summary and Conclusion

This chapter has reviewed civil rights legislation and relevant Supreme Court cases. A number of important affirmative action–based constructs (such as disparate-impact analysis, statistical-imbalance rationales, quotas, and layoffs) were discussed. From the preceding discussion, it quickly becomes evident that affirmative action poses complex legal issues. As a result, it is difficult to provide administrators with exact guidelines for implementation of affirmative action. Nevertheless, some general guidelines and cautions can be extracted from the cases analyzed. A university's race- and gender-based affirmative action programs should do the following ten things:

1. Identify and articulate needs for greater racial/ethnic minority and female participation or involvement
2. Design interventions to address *specific* identified needs
3. Be based on a plan that directly promotes a goal while simultaneously avoiding any harmful effects, to the extent possible
4. Be based on a precisely tailored, well-documented plan that is tied to the institution's own work force (or student body) by comparison with the relevant labor or talent pool
5. Avoid the use of strict numerical quotas based on race or gender
6. Implement race- and gender-based plans backed by statistical documentation

7. Promote flexible goals whereby all candidates compete for all openings, every qualified applicant is considered, and unqualified applicants are not admitted or hired merely to satisfy a goal
8. Be temporary and implemented only where color-blind efforts have failed to reach a stated goal
9. Avoid creating "innocent victims"
10. Keep in mind the program's economic feasibility for the institution.

The legal side of affirmative action is complex and ever changing. Just as the 1988 Supreme Court term reversed some earlier, race-conscious trends, future court decisions may modify and reverse these recent rulings. Therefore, student affairs administrators and all university personnel should not rely solely on the latest case in deciding affirmative action policy; rather, they must be constantly vigilant in attempts to develop innovative and creative interventions aimed at pluralizing the campus environment. As Doris J. Wright emphasizes in Chapter Six, universities must act autonomously, to some degree, in their attempts to facilitate an academic community that is in the best interests of society. (Portions of Chapters Four and Five and all of Chapter Six provide some ideas directed toward this goal.)

A final point that must be emphasized is the complexity and ever changing status of affirmative action case law. To this end, we conclude our discussion with a final recommendation: each student affairs unit should have its own affirmative action committee, composed of a multicultural (across race, gender, handicap) group. Such a committee should be responsible for keeping track of the latest affirmative action developments related to its own unit. The committee should have a direct channel to the university's legal experts on affirmative action, and it should meet regularly (at least once every two weeks) to discuss the current status of minority issues in the unit and to share recent literature on the topic. An understanding of legal responsibilities (for example, through information on updated court decisions and interpretations) and various intervention options can be one important focus of such a committee. Members would be responsible for informing the department head and the staff about recent developments and important issues. The committee should engage in regular evaluative research to assess procedures for minority recruitment, retention, and promotion. The committee could also serve as an advisory unit to all its departmental search-and-promotion committees. Membership on the committee must be rewarded (for example, with release time from other activities), and the administrative head must make it clear to the staff that this is an important committee whose suggestions and recommendations will be seriously considered and often implemented.

References

Adelman, R. W. "Voluntary Affirmative Action Plans by Public Employers: The Disparity in Standards Between Title VII and the Equal Protection Clause." *Fordham Law Review*, 1987, 56, 403–430.

Atkinson, D. R., Staso, D., and Hosford, R. "Selecting Counselor Trainees with Multicultural Strengths: A Solution to the Bakke Decision Crisis." *Personnel and Guidance Journal*, 1978, 56, 546-549.

Bales, J. "Burden of Proof Shifted to Plaintiff in Bias Case." *APA Monitor*, 1989a, 20 (8), 7.

Bales, J. "Hopkins Decision Tracks APA Brief." *APA Monitor*, 1989b, 2 (8), 36.

Barr, M. J. *Student Affairs and the Law*. New Directions for Student Services, no. 22. San Francisco: Jossey-Bass, 1983.

Barr, M. J. *Student Services and the Law: A Handbook for Practitioners*. San Francisco: Jossey-Bass, 1988.

Bersoff, D. N. "Should Subjective Employment Devices Be Scrutinized?" *American Psychologist*, 1988, 43 (12), 1016-1018.

Clague, M. W. "The Affirmative Action Showdown of 1986: Implications for Higher Education." *Journal of College and University Law*, 1987, 14 (2), 171-257.

Cox, P. N. *Employment Discrimination*. New York: Garland Law Publishing, 1988.

Dreyfuss, J. D., and Lawrence, C. *The Bakke Case: The Politics of Inequality*. San Diego, Calif.: Harcourt Brace Jovanovich, 1979.

Greenhouse, L. "Court Bars a Plan Set Up to Provide Jobs to Minorities." *New York Times*, Jan. 24, 1989a, pp. A1, A19.

Greenhouse, L. "Signal on Job Rights." *New York Times*, Jan. 25, 1989b, pp. A1, A18.

Lamber, J. "Observations on the Supreme Court's Recent Affirmative Action Cases." *Indiana Law Journal*, 1987, 62 (243), 243-261.

Lawrence, C. "Minority Issues in Higher Education." Paper presented at Haverford College, Haverford, Pa., Oct. 1988.

Morris, A. A. "Affirmative Action and 'Quota' Systems." *Education Law Reporter*, 1986, 28, 1203-1235.

Schwartz, B. *Constitutional Law: A Textbook*. New York: Macmillan, 1972.

Schwartz, B. *Behind Bakke: Affirmative Action and the Supreme Court*. New York: New York University Press, 1988.

Seaquist, G. "Civil Rights and Equal Access: When Laws Apply—and When They Do Not." In M. J. Barr (ed.), *Student Services and the Law: A Handbook for Practitioners*. San Francisco: Jossey-Bass, 1988.

Sexton, J. "Minority Admissions Program After Bakke." *Harvard Educational Review*, 1979, 49 (3), 313-339.

Tracey, T. J., and Sedlacek, W. E. "The Relationship of Noncognitive Variables to Academic Success: A Longitudinal Comparison by Race." *Journal of College Student Personnel*, 1985, 26 (5), 405-409.

Cases Cited

City of Richmond v. J. A. Croson Company, 57 U.S.L.W. 4132 (1989).

Firefighters Local Union #1784 v. Stotts, 467 U.S. 561 (1980).

Fullilove v. Klutznick, 448 U.S. 448 (1980).

Grove City College v. Bell, 465 U.S. 555 (1984).

Johnson v. Santa Clara County Transportation Agency, 480 U.S. (1987).

Local #28 of the Sheet Metal Workers' International Association v. Equal Employment Opportunity Commission, 478 U.S. 421 (1986).

Local #93, International Association of Firefighters v. City of Cleveland, 478 U.S. 501 (1986).

Martin v. Wilks, 57 U.S.L.W. 4616 (1989).

Patterson v. McLean Credit Union, 57 U.S.L.W. 4705 (1989).

Price Waterhouse v. Hopkins, 57 U.S.L.W. 4469 (1989).

Regents of the University of California v. Bakke, 438 U.S. 265 (1978).

United States v. Paradise, 480 U.S. 149 (1987).
United Steelworkers of America v. Weber, 443 U.S. 193 (1979).
Wards Cove Packing Company, Inc. v. Atonio, 57 U.S.L.W. 4583 (1989).
Watson v. Fort Worth Bank & Trust, 56 U.S.L.W. 4922 (1988).
West v. Atkins, 487 U.S. 101 L. Ed. 2d 40 (1988).
Wygant v. Jackson Board of Education, 476 U.S. 267 (1986).

Diane E. Lewis is a doctoral student in counseling psychology at Fordham University–Lincoln Center, New York.

Lindsay J. Lewis is an attorney for Sills Cummis Zuckerman Radin Tischman Epstein & Gross of Newark, New Jersey. He serves on the Board of Governors of the New York University Law Review Alumni Association, which in May 1990 organized the symposium "City of Richmond v. J. A. Croson: Implications for Affirmative Action."

Joseph G. Ponterotto is associate professor of counseling and counseling psychology, Division of Psychological and Educational Services, Graduate School of Education, Fordham University–Lincoln Center, New York.

A current examination of the status of racial/ethnic minorities in higher education reveals that affirmative action efforts are needed for recruiting and retaining culturally diverse students on campus.

Racial/Ethnic Minority and Women Students in Higher Education: A Status Report

Joseph G. Ponterotto

It has been twenty years since the crest of the civil rights movement, and now is a good time to assess the collective progress of institutions of higher education with respect to affirmative action efforts. Over the long run, has affirmative action been effective? What are the demographic data? Clearly, university administrators, faculty, and students have a responsibility to know the facts; otherwise, there is little chance that they will contribute efforts aimed at pluralizing the campus in terms of minority recruitment, curriculum expansion, and attitudinal change. The problem of minorities' presence and comfort on campus must be recognized and defined before it can be addressed.

This chapter presents a selective yet comprehensive status report on racial/ethnic minority and women students in higher education. The current educational status of these groups will be discussed, with greater attention given to racial/ethnic minorities. This chapter reviews the most recent data on general demographic trends, college enrollments, graduate rates, and attrition rates, disaggregated by race and gender. The importance of campus climate to the retention of racial/ethnic minority and women students is highlighted, and recommendations for improving campus climate are made.

Population Trends and Implications for Higher Education

Chapter One introduced the notion of the changing demographic face of America. It is important to underscore the fact that our society is in the

New Directions for Student Services, no. 52, Winter 1990 © Jossey-Bass Inc., Publishers

midst of a dramatic demographic shift, and to note the implications. Racial/ethnic minority persons currently make up 20 percent of the total U.S. population. By the year 2020, this percentage will jump to 34 percent (Hodgkinson, 1985); at some point during the twenty-first century, whites will become the numerical minority, constituting less than 50 percent of the total U.S. population (Ponterotto and Casas, forthcoming).

To understand the changing face of America, we must turn to an examination of trends in current and projected immigration (both legal and illegal) and fertility rates. Hodgkinson (1985), a leading population demographer, notes that to maintain its current numerical representation relative to the total population, a group must show a fertility rate of 2.1 children per female. The fertility rate for white women is currently 1.7 children, which signifies a decreasing white population. The fertility rate for black women is 2.4; for Puerto Rican women, 2.1; and for Mexican American women, 2.9. Collectively, the latter three groups will grow significantly in proportion to the white population. (The reader should note that not all Hispanic subgroups have higher-than-white fertility rates; Cuban Americans, for example, have a fertility rate of only 1.3 children per female, which presages an eventual decrease in the Cuban American population relative to the groups just mentioned.)

Another indicator of patterns in population growth is the relative youth of a given population. The average age of whites in America is thirty-one; of blacks, twenty-five; and of Hispanics, only twenty-two (Hodgkinson, 1985). Obviously, a major implication of these data is that the average Hispanic woman is just moving into the peak childbearing years, while the average white woman is moving out of them. Another important data set of interest to college administrators is the eighteen-to-twenty-four-year-old cohort, the traditional backbone of college enrollments. It is significant that 39.5 percent of whites, 42.3 percent of Asians, 50.3 percent of blacks, 53.9 percent of Hispanics, and 54.3 percent of Native Americans are now under the age of twenty-five (U.S. Census data cited in Ponterotto and Casas, forthcoming). Thus, Ponce (1988) notes that by the year 2020, racial/ethnic minorities will comprise 40 percent of the eighteen-to-twenty-four-year-old population.

A final indicator of population demographics is current and projected immigration trends. The 1980s have witnessed, and the 1990s will continue to witness, increased immigration from Southeast Asia and from South and Central America (National Council of La Raza, 1987). There is little doubt that an important challenge—if not the major one—to institutions of higher education will be to adjust to the realities of a truly multiracial, multicultural society. Few would argue that there is moral, ethical, and legal pressure on colleges and universities to provide equal educational opportunity (meaning both institutional access and retention) to currently underrepresented racial/ethnic groups. Equally important is higher education's responsibility to the current cultural majority—white students—who are not being prepared to enter a culturally diverse world. Unfortunately, on some predominantly white campuses, a majority student (or a racial/ethnic minority student, for that matter) can proceed through an entire four-year curriculum without ever taking a course from a black or Hispanic professor. Inadequate exposure to culturally diverse campus personnel is probably as much an educational disservice to white students as it is to racial/ethnic minority students.

In addition to society's moral responsibility to educate all Americans, there is a fiscal reality that many institutions—particularly private, tuition-dependent colleges—will soon face: unless universities can attract today's nontraditional students (elderly people, culturally diverse students, and people with disabilities, for example), many institutions will face financial collapse (see Cardoza, 1986; Wright, 1987).

Racial/Ethnic Minority and Female Enrollment in Higher Education

Two major tools for estimating the number of racial/ethnic minority students enrolled in higher education are the national surveys of households conducted by the U.S. Census Bureau and the U.S. Department of Education's direct survey (conducted every two years) of colleges, conducted for its Office of Civil Rights. According to the specific data-collection method, figures may vary somewhat. Moreover, there is a three-year lag from the time data are collected until they are analyzed, organized, and disseminated in official reports. As of September 1989, the most recent figures in college enrollment are from 1986. Sometime during late 1990, new figures will be released, covering data from 1988.

This section briefly and selectively reviews the most current demographic enrollment data for postsecondary institutions. The majority of these data have been summarized from three basic sources: American Council on Education (1988), U.S. Department of Education (1988), and Commission on Minority Participation in Education and American Life (1988).

High School Completion Rates. From 1976 to 1986, high school completion rates increased for the total population and for each of the three largest racial/ethnic groups. In 1976, 80.5 percent of Americans between eighteen and twenty-four years old had completed high school; by 1986, this figure had climbed to 82.1 percent. High school graduate rates for whites rose, from 82.4 percent to 83.1 percent, during this ten-year period. High school graduation rates for blacks underwent the greatest increase during this time, rising from 67.5 percent (1976) to 76.4 percent (1986). Hispanic completion rates also rose during this period, from 55.6 percent to 57.9 percent (American Council on Education, 1988).

General College Enrollments. College enrollment data for high school graduates between eighteen and twenty-four indicate that total enrollment increased, from 33.1 percent (1976) to 34.0 percent (1986). During this time, the percentage of the white population that was enrolled in college also increased, from 33.0 percent (1976) to 34.1 percent (1986). Parallel figures for blacks reveal a decrease in college enrollments, from 33.4 percent (1976) to 28.6 percent (1986). Hispanic enrollments for this age group also showed decline, from 35.8 percent (1976) to 29.4 percent (1986).

These figures are quite alarming in that black and Hispanic youths' college enrollment is decreasing, despite their increasing high school graduation rates. Broadening this examination somewhat, to include persons twenty-four years old or younger who are enrolled in college *or* who have completed one or more years of college, we note that from 1975 to 1986 the percentage of whites in this category increased, from 53 percent to 55 percent. The rate for blacks decreased during this period, from 48 percent to 46 percent, as did the rate for Hispanics, falling from 51 percent to 45 percent (Commission on Minority Participation in Education and American Life, 1988).

Table 1 presents a comprehensive breakdown of college and university enrollments by race, from 1978 to 1986. Actual numerical enrollments, as well as percentages of total enrollment, are shown. The table reveals that Native American enrollments have increased marginally, in raw numbers, but Native Americans still make up fewer than 1 percent of students. Asian American enrollments have grown significantly, representing 2.1 percent of 1978 enrollments and 3.6 percent of 1986 enrollments. Black enrollments increased marginally, from 1.076 million in 1984 to 1.081 million in 1986, but this number is lower than the 1980 total of 1.107 million. Blacks, who constituted over 9 percent of all college students in 1978 and 1980, made up only 8.6 percent of all students enrolled in 1986. Hispanic enrollments have increased, reaching the 5 percent mark in 1986. The white student body, although it increased numerically from 1984 to 1986, has decreased in total percentage of enrollments, falling to 79.3 percent in 1986.

Two points are particularly important in interpreting Table 1. First, the total American racial/ethnic minority population (not counting foreign students) has increased steadily, although slowly, and now represents 17.9 percent of the college population. This percentage is far below the percentage of racial/ethnic minorities in society generally, which is now over 20 percent. Further, given the general youthfulness of the racial/ethnic minority population, with a higher concentration of eighteen-to-twenty-four-year-olds than is indicated by the 20 percent aggregate representation estimate, the racial/ethnic minority participation rates reported in Table 1 become even more disparate. Second, there is disparity in college enrollment among specific racial/ethnic minority groups. While Asian Americans (and, to some extent, Hispanics, although we must keep in mind their accelerated growth relative to all other ethnic groups) increasingly are seen

Table 1. College and University Enrollments by Racial/Ethnic Group, 1978-1986 (in Numbers [Thousands] and Percentages)

| | Year | | | | |
Racial/Ethnic Group	1978	1980	1982	1984	1986
Native American					
Number	78	84	88	84	90
Percentage	.70	.70	.70	.69	.72
Asian American					
Number	235	286	351	390	448
Percentage	2.1	2.4	2.8	3.2	3.6
Black					
Number	1054	1107	1101	1076	1081
Percentage	9.4	9.2	8.9	8.8	8.6
Hispanic					
Number	417	472	519	535	624
Percentage	3.7	3.9	4.2	4.4	5.0
Total Minority					
Number	1784	1949	2059	2085	2243
Percentage	15.9	16.2	16.6	17.1	17.9
White					
Number	9194	9833	9997	9815	9914
Percentage	81.9	81.4	80.7	80.2	79.3
Foreign					
Number	253	305	331	335	344
Percentage	2.3	2.5	2.7	2.7	2.8
Total Enrollment	11231	12087	12387	12235	12501

Note: Enrollment data are for private and public colleges, two-year colleges, and undergraduate, graduate, and professional students. Data are based on a survey conducted by the U.S. Department of Education. This table is a synthesis of information presented in the *Chronicle of Higher Education,* July 6, 1988, pp. 20-29.

on college campuses, the situation for Native Americans has not improved, and the situation for blacks has actually worsened.

Table 2 examines the enrollment figures for 1986 more closely. This assessment includes an overview across race, gender, type of institution, and degree program. It is important for student administrators to have a general grasp of this information, since it has direct bearing on affirmative action efforts.

That women students are now the numerical majority on campus is clear from the first row of Table 2. With the exception of the Asian American and foreign student groups, the percentage of women is higher for all racial/ethnic groups. Also of particular interest in Table 2 is the fact that Hispanics and Native Americans are apparently more likely to be en-

Table 2. 1986 Enrollment by Racial/Ethnic Group, Gender, and Type of Institution (in Numbers [Thousands] and Percentages)

| | | | | | | | Racial/Ethnic Group | | | | | |
| | Native American | | Asian American | | Black | | Hispanic | | White | | Foreign | |
Category	Number	%	Number	%	Number	%	Number	%	Number	%	Number	%
Men	40	44.7	239	53.3	436	40.3	292	46.8	4646	46.9	232	67.4
Women	51	56.7	209	46.7	645	59.7	332	53.2	5268	53.1	111	32.3
Public	79	87.8	372	83.0	855	79.1	539	86.4	7650	77.2	226	65.7
Private	11	12.2	76	17.0	226	20.9	84	13.5	2264	22.8	118	34.3
Four-year	40	44.4	262	58.5	615	56.9	278	44.6	6340	63.9	291	84.6
Two-year	51	56.7	186	41.5	466	43.1	345	55.3	3575	36.1	53	15.4
Undergraduate	84	93.3	394	87.9	995	92.0	569	91.2	8552	86.3	204	59.3
Graduate	5	5.6	43	9.6	72	6.7	46	7.4	1132	11.4	136	39.5
Professional	1	1.1	11	2.5	14	1.3	9	1.4	230	2.3	4	1.2
Total	90		448		1081		624		9914		344	

Note: Information synthesized from Chronicle of Higher Education, July 6, 1988, pp. 20–29. Because of rounding, percentages may not add up to 100 in all cases.

rolled in two-year colleges. Given that the "pipeline" from two-year colleges to four-year institutions has not worked very well for racial/ethnic minorities in general (see Richardson and Bender, 1987), the implications of these data are clear for joint four-year college–two-year college affirmative action efforts.

Undergraduate Enrollments. Table 3 (synthesized from American Council on Education, 1988) shows enrollments from 1976 to 1986 for undergraduates only (Table 1 included graduate and professional students). Table 3 indicates that racial/ethnic minority enrollments have grown slowly, from a low of 16.3 percent in 1976 to a high of 18.9 percent in 1986. This increase is due primarily to the growth of Asian American and Hispanic enrollments. Native American enrollments have hovered around 0.7 percent, and black enrollments decreased, from a high of 10.0 percent in 1976–1978 to a low of 9.2 percent in 1986.

Graduate School Enrollments. In examining graduate school enrollments disaggregated by racial/ethnic group, we see a similar trend (data not shown in Table 3). Overall, the share of racial/ethnic minority students rose slowly, from 9.8 percent in 1976 to 11.6 percent in 1986. Again, this aggregate rise was due primarily to Hispanics, whose numbers increased from 1.8 percent in 1976 to 3.2 percent in 1986, and to Asian Americans, who increased from 1.7 percent to 3.0 percent during the same period. Black enrollments in graduate school decreased, from a high of 5.9 percent in 1978 to 5.0 percent in 1986. Throughout the same period, Native American enrollments in graduate school remained steady at 0.4 percent.

Professional School Enrollments. When we look specifically at professional school enrollments (not shown in Table 3), the figures appear somewhat more encouraging for culturally diverse students. Total racial/ethnic minority enrollments increased, from 8.6 percent in 1976 to 13.2 percent in 1986. During this period, black enrollments increased from 4.6 percent

Table 3. Undergraduate Enrollment in Higher Education by Race/Ethnicity, Fall 1976 to Fall 1986 (Percentage Distribution)

Racial/Ethnic Group	Year					
	1976	1978	1980	1982	1984	1986
White, non-Hispanic	82.2	81.4	81.0	80.5	80.0	79.2
Total minority	16.3	16.8	17.0	17.5	18.0	18.9
Black, non-Hispanic	10.0	10.0	9.7	9.4	9.4	9.2
Hispanic	3.7	4.0	4.1	4.5	4.7	5.3
Asian American	1.8	2.1	2.4	2.9	3.2	3.6
Native American	0.7	0.7	0.7	0.8	0.7	0.8
Foreign	1.5	1.7	2.0	2.0	2.0	1.9

Note: Information synthesized from American Council on Education (1988, Table 5, p 26). Because of rounding, percentages may not add up to 100 in all cases.

to 5.2 percent, Hispanic enrollments from 1.9 percent to 3.4 percent, and Asian American enrollments from 1.7 percent to 4.2 percent. Again, however, Native American enrollments showed no gain; indeed, they fell, from 0.5 percent in 1976 to 0.4 percent in 1986. White enrollments in professional schools have declined slowly, from a high of 90.1 percent in 1976 to a low of 85.2 percent in 1986.

Update. Although the most current national data base on student enrollment is derived from 1986 figures, there are national survey data on changes taking place from year to year. El-Khawas (1988) surveyed senior administrators at 367 colleges and universities (including two-year colleges, baccalaureate colleges, comprehensive universities, and doctoral institutions). Findings of this survey most relevant to the present discussion are as follows: 54 percent of the institutions showed general enrollment increases since 1980, the majority reporting enrollment gains specifically for the 1987–1988 academic year, while 55 percent of the independent institutions and 53 percent of the public four-year colleges reported increases in the share of costs that students and parents had to pay. Specifically, with respect to racial/ethnic minority enrollments, roughly 25 percent of the institutions increased their enrollments of blacks, Hispanics, or Asian American students, and 15 percent reported increased enrollment of Native American students. Roughly 67 percent of the administrators rated their institutions' performance in attracting racial/ethnic minority students as fair or poor (as opposed to excellent or very good). With respect to retaining enrolled black and Hispanic students, approximately 40 percent assigned ratings of poor or fair to their institutions (see El-Khawas, 1988, for an extended discussion).

Racial/Ethnic Minority Student Attrition

Clearly, a first step in campus affirmative action efforts is to increase the numbers of racial/ethnic minority students who enroll. A second and equally important step is to keep students enrolled until they graduate. Figures on student attrition vary widely according to type and size of surveys, regions where surveys are conducted, and methods of analyzing survey data. Regardless of the methods or mechanisms for collecting attrition-rate data, however, one trend is unequivocal: members of some racial/ethnic groups are much more likely than others to leave college before graduation.

Wilson and Justiz (1987/1988) review data showing that, of 1980 high school graduates who entered college, 26 percent of white students, 28 percent of Mexican American students, 28 percent of Native American students, 31 percent of black students, and 42 percent of Puerto Rican students had dropped out by February 1984. The American Council on Education (1988) documents that, of the 1980 high school graduates who had entered college by 1982, 47 percent of Asian Americans, 55 percent of whites, 65 percent of Native Americans, 66 percent of Hispanics, and 71 percent of blacks had left school by 1986 without completing their baccalaureate degrees.

Retaining Racial/Ethnic Minority Students

Why do racial/ethnic minority groups (particularly blacks, Hispanics, and Native Americans) drop out of college at higher rates than whites do? A number of reasons are repeatedly cited in the literature: declining financial aid, lack of a definitive relationship between a college degree and a good job, inadequate high school guidance programs, attraction to the military for high-tech education, institutional racism, increased racial tension on campus, lack of a significant pool of racial/ethnic role models, and minorities' isolation on campus (see discussions by Hodgkinson, 1985; Ponce, 1988; Wilson and Justiz, 1987/1988).

From an extensive body of literature on racial/ethnic minority dropout trends, there emerges a key summative factor, best described as the *campus climate*. This term refers to the academic, social, and interpersonal comfort that racial/ethnic minorities feel on campus. Green (1988, p. 13) defines campus climate as embracing "the culture, habits, decisions, practices, and policies that make up campus life. It is the sum total of the daily environment, and central to the comfort factor that minority students, faculty, staff, and administrators experience on campus. Students, and other members of the campus community who feel unwelcome or alienated from the mainstream of campus life are unlikely to remain. If they do remain, they are unlikely to be successful."

For many racial/ethnic minorities on predominantly white campuses, the climate is not hospitable. Racial/ethnic minority students report feeling recruited and tolerated but not really appreciated from a cultural perspective (see Ponterotto, Martinez, and Hayden, 1986). Although the lack of hospitality is sometimes manifested overtly, as in acts motivated by racism and increasing incidents of racial confrontation (see Green, 1988; Wilson and Justiz, 1987/1988), more often than not it is demonstrated in more subtle ways. For example, a university fraternity organizes a "slave auction" to raise money for disadvantaged children. Brothers in the fraternity (black and white) are auctioned off to the highest bidder (the audience is composed mostly of women from sororities) for an evening's dinner and date. Or again, a fraternity advertising an upcoming party posts flyers all over the campus. The flyers feature pictures of naked women. What impact do these events have on the campus climate for nonwhite and female students and staff? What should the student affairs administrator's response be to these events? Where do each of these cases fall on the border between free speech and racial or sexual insensitivity? What interventions could be used to educate the parties involved about the harmful emotional impact of these actions?

On a more general level, there are two important factors involved in campus climate: the institutionally accepted value system, and the existing minority representation on campus. A subtle aspect of the first factor concerns the appreciation of culturally diverse value systems and emphases. Clearly, the value system inherent in today's predominantly white universities is the white middle-class value system of western European origin (see Katz, 1985; Wilkerson, 1989). White cultural values—such as rigid schedules, a competitive nature, and individual achievement and autonomy—are not universally accepted. Students from some racial/ethnic groups (for example, traditional Native American students and minimally acculturated Mexican American students) may be more oriented toward flexible schedules, cooperative effort, and group achievement. With respect to the second important factor in campus climate, being a member of a minority group on campus is stressful, and this is true regardless of how internally secure and self-confident a person may be.

Improving the Campus Climate

Appreciating Cultural Diversity. If the campus climate is more hospitable, as manifested in understanding of and expressed appreciation for racial/ethnic cultural variations in value systems and emphases, then the minority student is more likely to stay in school and graduate (see Green, 1988). The first step in improving the campus climate is to educate the university community about how it is currently not hospitable to minorities. Most white males on campuses do not understand how the campus climate can be a negative influence on many women and racial/ethnic minority students. Surveys consistently show that the white majority on predominantly white campuses is likely to believe that conditions for nonwhites are no worse than they are for whites (see discussions by Beckham, 1987/1988; Green, 1988). A crucial step, then, is to educate the majority about the ethnocentric cultural bias on campus. Three brief examples of ethnocentrism are presented here, to clarify the manifestation of this sort of value bias.

Nonverbal Behavior. Appropriate nonverbal communication patterns are predicated by culture, to some degree. For example, white middle-class people (especially men) are expected to maintain eye contact during a conversation and to offer a firm handshake. If a Native American student does not maintain eye contact with a professor during a classroom interaction, how is this behavior interpreted? Is the professor culturally sensitive enough to know that this may be a sign of respect for an authority figure? Or will the professor interpret this behavior as the student's resistance or lack of motivation?

Individual Achievement. The university culture, serving as an extension of the white middle-class male culture with its western European roots, fosters an emphasis on individuation and autonomy (see Katz, 1985). Raising one's hand in class and thereby drawing attention to oneself is a valued trait in the campus environment. A traditional Native American or a traditional Mexican American student may not be willing to raise his or her hand in class (even if he or she knows the answer) because drawing attention to oneself may not be a culturally valued attribute. Again, there is no right or wrong value system; the issue is one of cultural understanding. Will the behavior of this hypothetical Native American or Mexican American student be misinterpreted as lack of interest or as not being prepared for class?

Competition. Is the classroom environment one of competition, manifested by an emphasis on individual achievement and individualized tests? Are the desks set up in rows and columns, emphasizing individuation and autonomy, or are they arranged in a circle, emphasizing group cohesion? A number of racial/ethnic cultures clearly do not place a high value on the white middle-class male ideal of being fiercely competitive. Students from some minority groups seem to do much better on group projects and collaborative efforts (see Aaronson and Yates, 1983).

The entire campus community (majority and racial/ethnic minority students) must be educated about the various value systems represented on campus and about the tendency to expect culturally diverse students to adapt to a single value system (see Pounds, 1987, on the need for racial/ethnic minorities also to undergo such training). The entire university community should understand that the campus is markedly enriched when cultural diversity is understood, appreciated, and shared. The real world is culturally pluralistic, and the campus atmosphere should reflect this reality.

Although the student affairs literature is replete with specific suggestions on mechanisms for educating the campus community with respect to cultural understanding (for example, lectures and films, "awareness" weeks, status reports, and so on), my suggestion is that all incoming freshmen and transfer students be required to take a full-semester course (carefully planned and designed) on a topic such as the richness of cultural diversity on and off campus. All student services units should also participate in similar workshops and continuing education.

In the past, vast amounts of energy and money have been allocated to special programs for at-risk students (many of them racial/ethnic minorities) and for development of counseling, tutoring, and orientation sessions. Although many of these programs have been successes, most have not had a collective or significant impact on campus climate. Energy and resources must also be devoted to continuing education for all current students, staff, and faculty.

It is important not to direct all efforts toward working with racial/ethnic minority students and helping them adjust to the campus's value system; such an emphasis conveys the subtle message that one value system is best. Instead of expecting (and, in fact, forcing) culturally diverse students to adopt the middle-class white male value system that dominates the campus (see Pearson, Shavlik, and Touchton, 1989), would it not be better to help campuses become culturally pluralistic or multicultural, so that people with various value systems can thrive on campus? Pounds (1987) emphasizes that the majority and the racial/ethnic minority communities alike should work toward becoming multicultural—that is, racial/ethnic minority students should adjust to the campus, to some degree, and the campus culture should adjust to culturally diverse groups.

How can the majority and racial/ethnic minority cultures work together to create a more multicultural campus atmosphere? First, rigidity and urgency with respect to time is an emphasis of the white middle-class culture (see Katz, 1985) that is clearly reflected throughout the campus environment. Time is viewed as linear; being on time and completing assignments on time is an important (and, in fact, a mandatory) value on campus. Some cultures view time as circular (for example, some Native American cultures), and rigid adherence to schedules is alien to them. Some Hispanic subgroups also put less emphasis on time than the white middle-class culture does. Culturally pluralizing the campus from the standpoint of time could mean considering flexible application deadlines, flexible assignment-completion dates, flexible (walk-in) office hours for faculty, untimed tests, and so on. (Naturally, all students should also be made aware of the importance of time in various careers.)

Second, the majority culture emphasizes the written tradition over the oral tradition. Most classes involve written tests and term papers, but some cultures (for example, the traditional Native American and black American cultures) emphasize oral history and oral storytelling from early childhood on (see Ponterotto and Casas, forthcoming). A culturally pluralistic class environment may be one where half of the student's grade is based on written assignments and half is based on oral presentations. (With high-enrollment classes, of course, such an intervention would be more difficult.)

Third, assertiveness is a valued and acceptable trait in the majority culture. Thus, if a student does not understand an assignment or a grade, it is deemed appropriate to approach the professor for clarification. In some racial/ethnic subgroups where the knowledge and wisdom of an authority figure is never questioned (for example, in some Asian American groups), it would seem insulting to approach a professor. Such an action would be seen as challenging the professor's wisdom or the clarity of his or her instructions. Therefore, students from some racial/ethnic groups may not feel at all comfortable approaching professors or teaching assistants. University faculty and administrators must be sensitive to how people from various cultures understand the student-professor or department head-staff member relationship. In some instances, professors or student administrators could approach students or employees to initiate consultation.

These brief examples highlight how racial/ethnic minority students can respond and adapt to the majority value system on campus and how the majority culture can simultaneously respond from a more pluralistic perspective. The campus that acknowledges and accepts a variety of value emphases sends the subtle yet powerful message that all students are equally valued and appreciated.

Increasing Racial/Ethnic Minority Representation. As we have seen, a crucial component of the welcoming campus climate is the existing racial/ethnic minority representation on campus. A university can have hundreds of lectures, films, and presidential statements on affirmative action, but if racial/ethnic minorities are not significantly visible on campus, the campus climate will not be hospitable to culturally diverse students. To attract racial/ethnic minority applicants and enrollees, and to increase retention rates for these students, a critical mass of racial/ethnic minorities must exist on campus. Green (1988) defines *critical mass* as 30 percent of the population, and she notes that research supports this figure with respect to the success of racial/ethnic minority students. A number of predominantly white schools, through rigorous and aggressive recruitment, are approaching this critical mass (Hodgkinson, 1985), but most are falling far short.

Recruiting large numbers of culturally diverse students is possible (numerous excellent sources on how to do it are available and are abstracted in Chapter Seven), if leaders are committed and if it becomes the university's priority. I have been continually amazed at how my two alma maters (one a small private college, the other a major public university) have been able, over two to five years, to raise millions of dollars for new buildings and other facilities. The commitment was there, and everyone, from the university president to the college freshmen, was involved in the funding drive. If this same commitment and energy were devoted to racial/ethnic minority student recruitment over a specified period, the numbers could increase dramatically; after all, more and more racial/ethnic minority students graduate from high school, and increasing numbers of adult minority students are willing to return to college. If we can enroll more racial/ethnic minority students, and if we can educate our campus communities to appreciate cultural plurality and demonstrate their appreciation (for example, by changing curricula), then the retention problem will begin to take care of itself.

Conclusion

The implications of the demographic and educational data presented in this chapter are important. Continued underrepresentation of racial/ethnic minorities in higher education will result in a growing economic schism between whites and nonwhites, and there will be more racial misunderstanding and violence, both on campus and off. A longer-term implication is that a growing segment of the population will not get the opportunity to fully contribute its intellectual resources to a highly advancing technological society. Economically, without greater numbers of racial/ethnic minority students, many colleges will go bankrupt and close, and the United States may not remain internationally competitive.

The campus climate for minorities must improve. If it does not, we will see increasing segregation on campus, higher racial/ethnic minority dropout rates due to alienation, and increased racial misunderstanding and stereotyping. If white males continue to see racial/ethnic minorities and women as a problem to deal with, instead of as culturally rich and campus-enhancing segments of the population, then polarization will intensify.

References

Aaronson, E., and Yates, S. "Cooperation in the Classroom: The Impact of the Jigsaw Method on Inter-Ethnic Relations, Classroom Performance, and Self-Esteem." In H. H. Blumberg, A. P. Hare, V. Kent, and M. Davies (eds.), *Small Groups and Social Interactions*. Vol. 1. New York: Wiley, 1983.

American Council on Education. *Minorities in Higher Education*. Washington, D.C.: American Council on Education, 1988.

Beckham, B. "Strangers in a Strange Land: Blacks on White Campuses." *Educational Record*, 1987/1988, 68 (4) and 69 (1), 74–78.

Cardoza, J. "Colleges Alerted: Pay Attention to Minorities—or Risk Future Survival." *ETS Developments*, 1986, 32 (2), 8–10.

Commission on Minority Participation in Education and American Life. *One-Third of a Nation*. Washington, D.C.: American Council on Education, Education Commission of the States, 1988.

El-Khawas, E. *Campus Trends, 1988*. Washington, D.C.: American Council on Education, 1988.

Green, M. F. (ed.). *Minorities on Campus: A Handbook for Enhancing Diversity*. Washington, D.C.: American Council on Education, 1988.

Hodgkinson, H. L. *All One System: Demographics of Education, Kindergarten Through Graduate School*. Washington, D.C.: Institute for Educational Leadership, 1985.

Katz, J. H. "The Sociopolitical Nature of Counseling." *Counseling Psychologist*, 1985, 13, 615–624.

National Council of La Raza. "Focus—The U.S. Hispanic Population: 1987." *Education Network News*, 1987, 6 (5), 1–12.

Pearson, C. S., Shavlik, D. L., and Touchton, J. G. (eds.). *Educating the Majority: Women Challenge Tradition in Higher Education*. New York: Macmillan, 1989.

Ponce, F. Q. "Minority Student Retention: Historical Beginnings." In M. C. Terrell and D. J. Wright (eds.), *From Survival to Success: Promoting Minority Student Retention*. Washington, D.C.: National Association of Student Personnel Administrators, 1988.

Ponterotto, J. G., and Casas, J. M. *Handbook of Racial/Ethnic Minority Counseling Research*. Springfield, Ill.: Thomas, in press.

Ponterotto, J. G., Martinez, F. M., and Hayden, D.C. "Student Affirmative Action Programs: A Help or Hindrance to Development of Minority Graduate Students?" *Journal of College Student Personnel*, 1986, 27 (4), 318–325.

Pounds, A. W. "Black Students' Needs on Predominantly White Campuses." In D. J. Wright (ed.), *Responding to the Needs of Today's Minority Students*. New Directions for Student Services, no. 38. San Francisco: Jossey-Bass, 1987.

Richardson, R. C., Jr., and Bender, L. W. *Fostering Minority Access and Achievement in Higher Education: The Role of Urban Community Colleges and Universities.* San Francisco: Jossey-Bass, 1987.

U.S. Department of Education. "1986 Minority Enrollment at 3,200 Institutions of Higher Education." *Chronicle of Higher Education,* 1988, *34* (43), 20-29.

Wilkerson, M. B. "Majority, Minority, and the Numbers Game." In C. S. Pearson, D. L. Shavlik, and J. G. Touchton (eds.), *Educating the Majority: Women Challenge Tradition in Higher Education.* New York: Macmillan, 1989.

Wilson, R., and Justiz, M. J. "Minorities in Higher Education: Confronting a Time Bomb." *Educational Record,* 1987/1988, *68* (4) and *69* (1), 8-15.

Wright, D. J. (ed.). *Responding to the Needs of Today's Minority Students.* New Directions for Student Services, no. 38. San Francisco: Jossey-Bass, 1987.

Joseph G. Ponterotto is associate professor of counseling and counseling psychology in the Division of Psychological and Educational Services, Graduate School of Education, Fordham University–Lincoln Center, New York.

Racial/ethnic minorities and women are underrepresented at most higher education administrative and faculty levels. The minority experience on campus is often a lonely and stressful one.

Racial/Ethnic Minority and Women Administrators and Faculty in Higher Education: A Status Report

Joseph G. Ponterotto

This chapter parallels Chapter Four in terms of format and purpose. Several key questions are also addressed in this chapter: What is the current status of racial/ethnic minorities and women in administrative and faculty positions? Have recent affirmative action efforts been successful in recruiting, retaining, and promoting racial/ethnic minorities and women as higher education leaders?

The astute and progressive administrator will have a solid grounding in the facts of how many minority persons are at his or her university and in the nation at large. Documented discrepancies between actual numbers of minorities on campus and in the labor pool provide both a legal and a moral rationale for affirmative action.

This chapter presents a recent status report on racial/ethnic minorities and women in higher education administration and faculty positions. The minority experience on campus is profiled, and specific stressors and challenges to minority staff and faculty are highlighted. The chapter concludes with specific recommendations directed toward the recruitment of racial/ethnic minorities and women.

Minority Representation in Higher Education Administration

With respect to minority administrators in higher education, an examination of Table 1 reveals a number of interesting trends. The proportion of women administrators has increased, from a total of 23.0 percent in 1975 to 35.1 percent in 1985, while the number of male administrators has decreased correspondingly, from 77.0 percent in 1975 to 64.9 percent in 1985. Total racial/ethnic minority representation in higher education administration has risen, from 9.2 percent in 1975 to 11.6 percent in 1985. A gender breakdown reveals that most of this increase was due to increases in female representation: racial/ethnic minority women were 2.9 percent of administrators in 1975 and 4.7 percent in 1985, whereas racial/ethnic minority males showed only a slight corresponding increase, from 6.3 percent in 1975 to 6.8 percent in 1985.

Black representation in administration has also increased, from 7.0 percent in 1975 to 7.6 percent in 1985. Most of this rise was also due to increases in female representation, from 2.3 percent in 1975 to 3.4 percent

Table 1. Full-Time Administrators in Higher Education by Race/Ethnicity and Sex, 1975, 1983, and 1985

| Race/Ethnicity and Sex | Year (Actual Numbers and Percentages) | | | | | |
| | 1975 | | 1983 | | 1985 | |
	Number	%	Number	%	Number	%
Total	96,924	100	117,486	100	124,374	100
Male	74,650	77.0	79,340	67.5	80,676	64.9
Female	22,274	23.0	38,146	32.5	46,698	35.1
White	88,054	90.8	105,420	89.7	109,972	88.4
Male	68,551	70.7	72,126	61.4	72,204	58.1
Female	19,503	20.1	33,294	28.3	37,768	30.4
Total Minority	8,870	9.2	12,066	10.3	14,402	11.6
Male	6,099	6.3	7,214	6.1	8,472	6.8
Female	2,771	2.9	4,852	4.2	5,930	4.7
Black	6,801	7.0	8,362	7.1	9,446	7.6
Male	4,566	4.7	4,727	4.0	5,203	4.2
Female	2,235	2.3	3,635	3.1	4,243	3.4
Hispanic	1,203	1.2	2,040	1.7	2,490	2.0
Male	906	0.9	1,386	1.2	1,598	1.3
Female	297	0.3	654	0.6	892	0.7
Asian American	600	0.6	1,234	1.1	1,920	1.5
Male	413	0.4	790	0.7	1,279	1.0
Female	187	0.2	444	0.4	641	0.5
Native American	266	0.3	430	0.4	546	0.4
Male	214	0.2	311	0.3	392	0.3
Female	52	0.1	119	0.1	154	0.1

Note: Data synthesized from American Council on Education (1988, p. 36, Table 14). Because of rounding, percentages may not add up to 100 in all cases.

in 1985; black males actually showed a decrease during this time, from 4.7 percent in 1975 to 4.2 percent in 1985. This trend for black males parallels trends in their participation as students (see Chapter Four) and is cause for alarm. In fact, the American Council on Education (1988) has expressed special concern about black males' participation at all levels of higher education.

Hispanic representation among administrators has increased, from 1.2 percent in 1975 to 2.0 percent in 1985, with both males and females rising four-tenths of one percentage point. Asian Americans' representation has also increased, from 0.6 percent in 1975 to 1.5 percent in 1985, with the number for males increasing at twice the rate of those for females (0.6 percent versus 0.3 percent).

As in the rates for Native Americans' participation as students, there was virtually no growth in the rates for their participation as administrators over this period. Overall, their representation did rise slightly, from 0.3 percent in 1976 to 0.4 percent in 1985, but there was no increase whatsoever in the number of Native American women administrators.

Minority Representation at the Top. Who runs American colleges and universities? In the most comprehensive study to date, the Center for Leadership Development of the American Council on Education (Green, 1988a) surveyed chief executive officers at 2,105 higher education institutions. This survey covered the continental United States, as well as Puerto Rico and other U.S. territories, and it included two-year colleges, specialized institutions, baccalaureate colleges, comprehensive colleges and universities, and doctorate-granting universities. Predominantly white and predominantly black institutions were also surveyed. Among the findings most relevant to our discussion are the following:

- Ninety-three percent of the presidents were white, and 90 percent were male.
- Women and racial/ethnic minorities were particularly underrepresented in doctorate-granting institutions.
- Two percent of the predominantly white institutions were headed by blacks, and more than 50 percent of the black presidents headed historically black institutions.
- With respect to affirmative action, "the data do not indicate that special consideration is being given to recruiting women or minorities for presidencies" (Green, 1988a, p. 30), and many women presidents head single-sex colleges, just as many black presidents head historically or predominantly black institutions.

In the Boardroom. A 1985 study (the most recent available) of college and university governing boards (reported in Ranbom, 1987/1988) revealed that approximately 90 percent of trustees are white. Racial/ethnic minorities are better represented on governing boards of public institutions, where they constitute about 15 percent of trustees; at independent colleges, they constitute only 6 percent. Most of the racial/ethnic-related data on governing boards' composition has focused on blacks; a 1977-to-1985 trend analysis showed the percentage of black trustees increasing marginally, from 6.0 percent to 6.3 percent.

Minority Representation Among Faculty

The American Council on Education's (1988) seventh annual status report presents the most current statistics on racial/ethnic minority and female representation among higher education faculty. This report presents data from 1975 to 1985. Table 2 shows a comprehensive breakdown of faculty by gender and race in 1975, 1983, and 1985.

Table 2. Full-Time Faculty in Higher Education by Race/Ethnicity and Sex, 1975, 1983, and 1985 (in Actual Numbers [Thousands] and Percentages)

| Race/Ethnicity and Sex | Year (Numbers [times 1,000] and Percentages) | | | | | |
| | 1975 | | 1983 | | 1985 | |
	Number	%	Number	%	Number	%
Total	446.8	100	485.7	100	488.8	100
Male	336.4	75.3	356.6	73.4	354.2	72.5
Female	110.5	24.7	129.2	26.6	134.6	27.5
White	409.9	91.7	440.5	90.7	439.8	90.0
Male	312.3	69.9	326.2	67.1	321.0	65.7
Female	97.7	21.9	114.3	23.5	118.8	24.3
Total Minority	36.9	8.3	45.2	9.3	49.0	10.0
Male	24.1	5.4	30.4	6.3	33.2	6.8
Female	12.8	2.8	14.8	3.1	15.8	3.2
Black	19.7	4.4	19.6	4.0	20.3	4.1
Male	10.9	2.4	10.5	2.2	11.1	2.3
Female	8.9	2.0	9.0	1.9	9.2	1.9
Hispanic	6.3	1.4	7.5	1.5	8.1	1.7
Male	4.6	1.0	5.2	1.1	5.7	1.2
Female	1.8	0.4	2.2	0.5	2.4	0.5
Asian American	9.8	2.2	16.9	3.5	19.1	3.9
Male	7.8	1.8	13.7	2.8	15.3	3.1
Female	1.9	0.4	3.2	0.7	3.8	0.8
Native American	1.1	0.2	1.3	0.3	1.6	0.3
Male	0.8	0.2	1.0	0.2	1.2	0.2
Female	0.3	0.1	0.4	0.1	0.4	0.1

Note: Data synthesized from American Council on Education (1988, p. 32, Table 11). Because of rounding, percentages may not add up to 100 in all cases.

From 1975 to 1985, the proportion of female faculty increased, from 24.7 percent to 27.5 percent; males showed a decrease during this time, from 75.3 percent to 72.5 percent. The number of white male faculty dropped from 69.9 percent in 1975 to 65.7 percent in 1985. White females increased their number, from 21.9 percent to 24.3 percent.

Overall, racial/ethnic minority representation on U.S. faculties rose, from 8.3 percent in 1975 to 10.0 percent in 1985. Males accounted for most of this growth, their numbers increasing by 1.4 percent, while women showed only 0.4 percent growth during this period.

Blacks, although increasing slightly in actual numbers from 1975 to 1985, actually decreased in percentage of total faculty, from 4.4 percent to 4.1 percent. The percentage of black male faculty also decreased, from 2.4 percent to 2.3 percent, as did that of black female faculty, from 2.0 percent to 1.9 percent.

Hispanic representation on U.S. faculties increased only slightly, from 1.4 percent in 1975 to 1.7 percent in 1985; Hispanic males and females alike showed only slight increase. These data are alarming, given the accelerated growth of the Hispanic population at large (see Chapters One and Four).

Asian Americans had the greatest specific gains among faculty members, jumping from 2.2 percent in 1975 to 3.9 percent in 1985. Increases among males accounted for the majority of growth in this group. Native American faculty, like Native American students and administrators, showed virtually no growth, although there were marginal increases in raw numbers. In 1976, Native Americans represented 0.2 percent of the U.S. faculty; in 1986, this figure stood at 0.3 percent.

Minority Faculty Representation, Disaggregated by Rank and Tenure

In examining minority representation rates among higher education faculty, it is important to consider the professional rank and tenure of the respective groups. Obviously, full professors and tenured faculty in general have significantly more power on campus, in terms of influencing administrative policy, selecting colleagues, and admitting graduate students. The following brief data profiles are synthesized from the American Council on Education's (1988) latest status report (this information is not reflected in Table 2).

Full Professors. In 1985, 88.3 percent of full professors were male and 11.7 percent were female. Whites constituted 92.7 percent of the group; blacks, 2.2 percent; Hispanics, 1.1 percent; Asian Americans, 3.7 percent; and Native Americans, 0.2 percent.

Associate Professors. 1985 data indicate the following figures for associate professors: 76.6 percent were male, and 23.4 percent were female. Whites represented 90.6 percent of the group; blacks, 3.7 percent; Hispanics, 1.6 percent; Asian Americans, 3.7 percent; and Native Americans, 0.4 percent.

Assistant Professors. In 1985, 64.2 percent of assistant professors were male, and 35.8 percent were female. Whites represented 87.5 percent of this cohort; blacks, 5.3 percent; Hispanics, 1.8 percent; Asian Americans, 5.0 percent; and Native Americans, 0.4 percent.

Instructors and Lecturers. Among all university instructors and lecturers in 1985, 57.8 percent were male, and 42.2 percent were female. Whites represented 87.8 percent of the group; blacks, 5.6 percent; Hispanics, 2.3 percent; Asian Americans, 3.8 percent; and Native Americans, 0.6 percent.

A close examination of these data reveals that whites and males are overrepresented at the higher ranks, and women and racial/ethnic minorities are (with the exception of the Asian American group) proportionally overrepresented at the lowest ranks.

Tenure. The overall percentage of tenured faculty rose, from 64.3 percent in 1975 to 71.1 percent in 1985. During this time, the number of tenured white faculty increased, from 65.3 percent to 72.0 percent; of blacks, from 47.8 percent to 61.7 percent; of Hispanics, from 53.8 percent to 67.1 percent; of Asian Americans, from 58.2 percent to 61.2 percent; and of Native Americans, from 53.3 percent to 64.9 percent.

Update. El-Khawas (1988) notes several changes from 1987 to 1988. Although approximately one-half of American colleges and universities reported net gains in the number of full-time faculty during the year, only 25 percent of these institutions reported a net gain among racial/ethnic minority faculty. Further, approximately one-half of the campuses reported no net changes in the number of women faculty, and 9 percent of the campuses reported net losses of women faculty members during the year.

Implications of Minority Underrepresentation

Minorities are underrepresented among senior administrators and tenured faculty for many of the same reasons why they are underrepresented among students. Predominantly white universities have not been perceived as hospitable and welcoming by many members of minority groups. There is a visible lack of minority role models on campus. Minorities are not part of the "word of mouth" network, and the white males in power have mixed feelings about how to react to more than token representation of minorities in senior leadership positions (see the interracial identity theory outlined by Helms, 1984, 1990).

There are many implications of minorities' holding only token jobs among academic leaders. Minority youth will not see higher education administration and teaching as promising careers. Current university personnel will not have the benefit of extensive multicultural contact and therefore will not even be aware of the need to broaden curricula and leadership styles. Negative racial/ethnic and gender stereotypes will be maintained and perpetuated. For administrators to facilitate affirmative action on their campuses, they must have a good grasp of the minority experience. Once university leaders are sensitive to minorities' needs and challenges, they will be in a good position to begin affirmative action interventions.

The Minority Experience on Campus: A Faculty and Staff Perspective

There is little doubt that subtle forms of racism and sexism pervade most predominantly white campuses (Association of American Colleges, 1986; Green, 1988b). Although most top university administrators and faculty have good intentions toward minority groups on campus, they may not be aware of the effects of some of their own behavior. In staff meetings, for example, women are more likely to be interrupted while speaking than men are (Association of American Colleges, 1986). Behavior like this can perpetuate sexism on campus. As we saw in Chapter Four, the need to educate all personnel about subtle racism and sexism is paramount in any institution's sincere affirmative action plan.

The numbers of racial/ethnic minority faculty and staff on campuses are even lower than the numbers of minority students. Predictably, the issue of campus climate, discussed with respect to students in Chapter Four, can also be taken up with respect to administrators and faculty. Belonging to a numerical minority among top administrators or faculty members entails unique challenges that white men have not experienced and therefore may not be aware of. Consider the following two statements taken from a report prepared as part of the Project on the Status and Education of Women (Association of American Colleges, 1986, p. 3): "When you're the first of your sex or your race in a position, three things apply to you. One—you're placed under a microscope. Two—you're allowed no margin for error. And three—the assumption is always made that you achieved your position on something other than merit. . . . The responsibilities of being an outsider on the inside are enormous. It often means that I am the only woman in whatever setting I find myself [in]. It means that I am often called upon to be *THE WOMAN*. I am asked to speak from the Woman's Perspective, as if I knew all women and their views."

Describing the experience of black faculty in predominantly white colleges, Moore (1987/1988, pp. 119–120) notes the subtle racism reflected in expectations for blacks: "Blacks are expected to be better in order to be equal. The black faculty member never gets off probation and must undergo a long series of separate proofs to demonstrate competence." Moore goes on to say (p. 121), "They exist in a fishbowl, having their competence and behavior routinely and unofficially evaluated by most of the persons with whom they come in contact. They feel that they are expected to be shining examples of civic virtue."

The Campus "Barrio." Other concerns expressed by minority faculty and staff revolve around the limited and proscribed role that they play on many campuses. Garza (1987/1988) discusses the "barrioization" and "ghettoization" of racial/ethnic minority faculty in predominantly white institutions. Describing mainly the status of Hispanic faculty, he notes that the majority are concentrated in certain departments (ethnic studies, Chicano studies, bilingual education, Spanish departments, and the like). Further, he says that Hispanic faculty's departmental and committee work is usually restricted to affirmative action–oriented committees and only rarely is solicited for powerful committees concerned with the larger campus (such as instructional, policy, and research committees).

Similarly, Green (1988b), describing the status of racial/ethnic minority administrators, notes that they are more likely to be clustered in equal opportunity programs, student services, and affirmative action programs. Minorities are also overrepresented in "soft-money, special services" positions, and many minority administrators seem to be assistants to other administrators.

That Lonely Feeling. Racial/ethnic minority faculty and administrators at predominantly white institutions, being few in number, often report feeling overworked, undervalued, and alienated (see Association of American Colleges, 1986; Exum, 1983; Garza, 1987/1988; Green, 1988b; Moore, 1987/1988). Minority faculty, who are more likely to be at the junior levels, often have heavy teaching loads, lack visible minority role models who could install a sense of vicarious belonging over the long run, lack proper mentoring in terms of tenure and promotion expectations, and face high demands for "minority services" and mentoring. Further, as Garza (1987/1988) notes, service activities and research programs that focus on minorities may not be as highly valued by tenure-granting faculty and administrators as more traditionally oriented service and research activities are. Therefore, it is not really surprising that most universities have had only slight success in recruiting and retaining minority faculty and administrators.

Improving the Status of Minorities on Campus

Efforts aimed at improving the representation and comfort of minority faculty and staff should parallel the same efforts with respect to students (see Chapter Four). Some minority faculty and administrators will come from the ranks of current students. To broaden the pool of applicants, universities must do a better job of welcoming and retaining minority students, yet to increase the comfort and retention of minority students, universities need more minority faculty and staff to serve as role models. Given this double bind, the affirmative action challenge to universities is great and implies the need for multifaceted interventions at all levels and ranks of institutions and in communities at large (see Casas's contribution in Chapter Six).

Improving the campus climate for racial/ethnic minority faculty and administrators involves understanding and appreciating cultural diversity and increasing the number of racial/ethnic minorities on campus. A first step involves educating all administrators, faculty, and students about the nature and magnitude of the problem and about the kinds of subtle and even unconscious behavior that make racial/ethnic minorities feel undervalued, misunderstood, and overworked.

Writing about the paucity of black faculty at predominantly white institutions, Moore (1987/1988, p. 117) notes the consistent findings of university task forces: "Each study one examines points to the attitudes and behavior of . . . white faculty as a major factor in the problem. Until the problem becomes a concern and interest of the white faculty, the number of black faculty will not change appreciably. For the fact is, most things change in a college or university when the faculty decides it wants them changed. The faculty members are the gatekeepers. They provide the advice and consent to the leadership. While a strong and committed administrative leadership can influence a faculty, as a general rule the faculty controls access to its ranks."

Mechanisms for creating cultural pluralism on campus were discussed in Chapter Four and are covered in detail in the sources briefly annotated in Chapter Seven. The remaining portion of this chapter focuses on specific steps for increasing the number of minority faculty and administrators on campus.

Recruiting Minority Administrators and Faculty

In some ways, recruiting a significant number of minority faculty and staff members poses an even greater challenge than recruiting minority students. After all, there is accelerated growth in the racial/ethnic minority youth population, and these young people are graduating from high schools at increasing rates. Nevertheless, the graduate-degree-holding racial/ethnic minority members willing to enter academia and higher education administration are simply too few. This situation calls for renewed vigorous and creative recruitment on the part of predominantly white universities. Predominantly white institutions should aim for a minimal 30 percent participation rate for racial/ethnic minorities on campus at all levels (vice-presidents, deans, department heads, and so on) within a specified period (say, ten to fifteen years).

First, for any affirmative action effort to be successful, there must be a clear message from the university's governing board and its president that the current level of minority representation on campus will no longer be tolerated. A widely disseminated policy report must accompany this commitment. Stanford University's recently released report is a comprehensive model (University Committee on Minority Issues, 1989).

Second, a central body or person must coordinate and follow up on the institution's intervention plan. This person or committee should have direct, immediate access to the president and should have a high level of institutional power and influence.

Third, an institutional audit will be necessary. I am often surprised, when I consult with various universities, at how poor their recordkeeping systems are with respect to the representation of racial/ethnic minorities, women, and people with disabilities in various departments and student service units. University personnel seem to be wary of recordkeeping, for fear of so-called reverse discrimination suits (see Yoshida, Cancelli, Sowinski, and Bernhardt, 1989). Nevertheless, one important factor in keeping race-conscious affirmative action within the law is the ability to statistically document how one's own pool of minority students or employees is disproportionate in terms of the available pool of applicants. Systematic, exact recordkeeping is an essential component of a well-coordinated affirmative action plan.

In any affirmative action intervention, the participants should be familiar with civil rights statutes and affirmative action case law (see Chapter Three), and they should have ready access to legal expertise on campus. With legal information at hand, one can set affirmative action plans into motion and run only minimal risk of a successful "reverse discrimination" lawsuit. On the subjects of recordkeeping, institutional audits, and goal-oriented timetables, an excellent source is Green (1988b). This book includes sample audit forms that can be adapted by specific departments and units.

General, well-intentioned affirmative action efforts will not be enough. Each faculty and student affairs unit must set a specific agenda and plan for recruitment efforts. I believe that specific percentage goals and time-tables are necessary to success (consider how a funding drive is organized for a new campus building). Legal counsel must advise every step of the way (for instance, goals must be flexible and temporary, and they should not involve strict quotas, set-asides, or layoffs; see Chapter Three).

The university's funding commitment to the affirmative action plan must be strong and sustained. Given that most university personnel respond well to reward systems, creative mechanisms can be used to reward units that are successful in recruiting minorities. Possibilities include an extra faculty-hiring line for a department, increased travel money for the counseling center staff, and so on. Again, as long as there is no aggrieved party (that is, as long as the whole department or unit will benefit), creative affirmative action efforts will be legal.

The applicant pool should be expanded, for administrative as well as faculty openings. It is advisable to work closely with professional organizations, such as the American College Personnel Association of the American Association for Counseling and Development, that maintain lists of female and racial/ethnic minority graduate students who wish to enter university administration. Predominantly black and female institutions should be considered in recruiting, rather than the "old boys' network." Corporations can be considered for recruitment and cooperative efforts. An institution should also keep track of its own minority graduates when considering new appointees. If a department has a "don't hire your own" policy, it should be examined closely. Does it make sense to let successful minority graduates go on to other schools or to corporations?

An institution should work closely with the larger minority community in its area. Minority communities are good networking sources. Minority community members could sit on all search committees.

"Necessary qualifications" should be defined carefully. Does excellence in the field include being able to relate to, mentor, and be a role model for minority students, or would this just be a nice extra in a candidate? For example, which of the following two candidates is more qualified for the job of full professor: a generally good teacher with seventy-three articles published in academic journals, or a generally good teacher with thirty-nine articles published and an exemplary reputation for mentoring minority students and attracting them to the campus? In this example, an important question is what constitutes a "qualified" candidate. Chapter Three emphasizes that admitting or hiring unqualified candidates is not an acceptable affirmative action mechanism, and justification for such an action would not withstand a "reverse discrimination" suit. But how qualified must one be? The first professor, according to the limited information presented, is competent in research and teaching. The second is competent in teaching, research (in most fields, thirty-nine publications would indicate research competence), and service. Since a qualified professor is generally one who demonstrates competence in teaching, research, and service, perhaps the second professor is the more qualified. One final point about this example: note that the race of neither candidate is listed. Although most departments need more minority faculty—and, legally, race, gender, and handicap can be used as "plus" factors in a hiring decision (see Chapter Three)—affirmative action ideals and pluralistic mentoring are required of all faculty.

The recruitment efforts of successful universities should be studied. Fortunately, we now have extensive descriptions of so-called model programs. In this vein, two excellent sources are Green (1988b) and Clewell and Ficklen (1986) (see also Moore, 1987/1988).

Conclusion

This chapter has examined the current status of minority administrators and faculty on campus. Although modest improvement can sometimes be documented, racial/ethnic minorities generally continue to be severely underrepresented among higher education faculty and administrators. A key ingredient of the successful recruitment and retention of minorities is the campus climate. The minority experience on campus is often a lonely and stressful one. Clearly, institutionwide affirmative action must confront the subtle forms of racism and sexism that pervade the college campus. Continuing education for all current personnel appears to be an important first step in creating a more hospitable campus environment for underrepresented groups. The data reviewed in this chapter support the need for renewed and vigorous affirmative action.

References

American Council on Education. *Minorities in Higher Education.* Washington, D.C.: American Council on Education, 1988.

Association of American Colleges. *The Campus Climate Revisited: Chilly for Women Faculty, Administrators, and Graduate Students.* Washington, D.C.: Association of American Colleges, 1986.

Clewell, B. C., and Ficklen, M. S. *Improving Minority Retention in Higher Education: A Search for Effective Institutional Practices.* Princeton, N.J.: Educational Testing Service, 1986.

El-Khawas, E. *Campus Trends, 1988.* Washington, D.C.: American Council on Education, 1988.

Exum, W. H. "Climbing the Crystal Stair: Values, Affirmative Action, and Minority Faculty." *Social Problems,* 1983, *30,* 383-389.

Garza, H. "The 'Barrioization' of Hispanic Faculty." *Educational Record,* 1987/1988, *68* (4) and *69* (1), 122-124.

Green, M. F. *The American College President: A Contemporary Profile.* Washington, D.C.: Center for Leadership Development, American Council on Education, 1988a.

Green, M. F. (ed.). *Minorities on Campus: A Handbook for Enhancing Diversity.* Washington, D.C.: American Council on Education, 1988b.

Helms, J. E. "Toward a Theoretical Explanation of the Effects of Race on Counseling: A Black/White Model." *Counseling Psychologist,* 1984, *12,* 4, 153-165.

Helms, J. E. *Black and White Racial Identity: Theory, Research, and Practice.* Westport, Conn.: Greenwood Press, 1990.

Moore, W., Jr. "Black Faculty in White Colleges: A Dream Deferred." *Educational Record,* 1987/1988, *68* (4) and *69* (1), 116-121.

Ranbom, S. "The Ivory Boardroom: A Closed Door for Minority Trustees." *Educational Record,* 1987/1988, *68* (4) and *69* (1), 125-126.

University Committee on Minority Issues. *Building a Multiracial, Multicultural University Community.* Stanford, Calif.: University Committee on Minority Issues, Stanford University, 1989.

Yoshida, R. K., Cancelli, A. A., Sowinski, J., and Bernhardt, R. "Differences in Information Sent to Minority and Non-Minority Prospective Applicants to Clinical, Counseling, and School Psychology Programs." *Professional Psychology: Research and Practice,* 1989, *20,* 179-184.

Joseph G. Ponterotto is associate professor of counseling and counseling psychology in the Division of Psychological and Educational Services, Graduate School of Education, Fordham University–Lincoln Center, New York.

Three experts on student development contribute their ideas on future directions for affirmative action.

Affirmative Action on Campus: Making It Work (Editors' Introduction)

Joseph G. Ponterotto, Diane E. Lewis, Robin Bullington

The goal of this chapter is to present a broader perspective on affirmative action. To help achieve this goal, three geographically dispersed practitioner-scientists present their thoughts and recommendations on affirmative action policy.

In the first segment, Robert D. Brown—distinguished professor, past president of the American College Personnel Association, and past two-term editor of the *Journal of College Student Development*—presents ideas on how professional organizations can enhance, monitor, and facilitate affirmative action goals on campus. He suggests interventions focusing on management policies within professional organizations, as well as those focusing on educational programming at large.

In the second segment, J. Manuel Casas, associate professor of education and senior associate of a leading Hispanic business-consulting firm, shows that if affirmative action efforts are to be successful, various factions within and outside the campus community must be cooperatively involved. He emphasizes the important role that faculty, outside funding and program-accreditation committees, and the corporate sector can play in a unified racial/ethnic minority–focused affirmative action effort.

Finally, Doris J. Wright, consultation program director and staff psychologist, warns that campus personnel must begin now to plan carefully if they wish to succeed in realizing the American ideal of equal educational opportunity for all. Focusing on racial/ethnic minorities, she emphasizes that educational excellence must not be seen as distinct from a culturally pluralistic learning environment. She notes that administrators must plan now for financial exigencies and personnel shortages, and they must reexamine their endowment practices.

Student affairs professional organizations can promote affirmative action goals through their strategies for management and educational programming.

Affirmative Action and Professional Associations: Useful Strategies

Robert D. Brown

Professional associations in higher education are in a powerful position to combat sexism and racism and to have an impact on recruitment, retention, and social acceptance of women and ethnic minorities (see the definition of *affirmative action* given in Chapter Two). This potential influence is extensive. Association members represent almost every college campus in the country; therefore, association newsletters reach an extensive network of individual professionals. These members are likely to be working in positions of relatively high authority and are also likely to be persons who influence the policies that affect the hiring and promotion of staff and the policies and practices that shape admission and retention programs. On larger campuses, and perhaps on smaller campuses as well, there are enough professionals to form a critical mass to develop support for new ideas and programs. Even professionals who are not all members of the same association are likely to find kindred spirits among their colleagues, who daily confront the same issues and make the same decisions.

The extent of this potential influence, particularly for student affairs professional associations, is campuswide. Association members may work in housing, admissions, campus activities, and counseling centers, as well as in deans' offices. Some may be faculty members who teach in training programs, and others may hold student affairs positions within specific academic colleges. What also makes student affairs professional associations unique is their focus: the student. By contrast, professional associations for history or math professors, for example, are composed of persons whose concerns focus primarily on their own disciplines. The history professor is often interested in history first and in teaching history second; and, although history's and teaching's impacts on the student are important, the student ranks third. For the student affairs professional, however, the success of students comes first—every student on campus, not just history or math majors. Thus, the student affairs professional has the opportunity and the interest to have an impact on students, as well as on professional colleagues.

It is important that association leaders be aware of this potential for broad power because with it comes an obligation: the valuable resources and networks that members of professional associations have available to them must not lie fallow. The challenge to forestall racism and sexism, and to develop among staff and students a strong sense of the value of diversity in higher education, will exist for some time to come. Certainly, the challenge is not only for student affairs professionals and their professional associations, but neglecting an opportunity to be a positive force on campuses across the country would mean failing to fulfill a moral obligation.

For student affairs professional associations to help the higher education community accomplish the goals of affirmative action, there must be a strategy, and there must be constant vigilance. The strategies that follow illustrate what a professional association can do—and there is much to do. They can be used as a stimulus or as a checklist for association leaders as they scrutinize their affirmative action efforts.

Strategies for Professional Associations to Promote Cultural Diversity

No one wants to suggest that professional associations have been negligent; all their efforts have been well intentioned, and they have accomplished much. Professional associations have been active partners in supporting the goals of affirmative action and promoting policies that positively affect the professional lives of women and minorities. Many of the examples of strategies given here were taken from existing programs. Too often, however, these efforts have been independent of one another, rather than parts of larger plans. The value of a plan or a strategy is that it can be goal-oriented: we can see where we have been and where we want to go, and we can map out a step-by-step process to get there. A plan also makes it possible to establish priorities.

The strategies discussed here are arbitrarily divided into two types: those that focus on management policies and practices within the professional association, and those that focus on educational programming. Management strategies, for the most part, are internal activities and most directly affect the association's leaders. Educational efforts can be targeted to association leaders (and thus can also be considered internal), but a significant number are also designed for members at large and for external audiences, such as faculty, staff colleagues, and students.

Management Policies and Practices

Four management dimensions illustrate strategies that the professional association can use to promote the goals of affirmative action: appointments, the budget process, election-slate decisions, and honors and awards.

Appointments. The most profound impact that American presidents have, according to many analysts, is felt through their appointments to the Supreme Court and other judicial bodies. The impact of appointments made within a professional association is hardly so profound, but such appointments can be important, and they can have impacts beyond an association president's official term. Key appointments (most of which must be approved by executive boards) include those of membership chairs, newsletter editors, journal editors, and members of editorial boards. Highly visible appointments also include those made to convention-planning teams and to ad hoc committees and special task forces. These roles provide individuals with opportunities to obtain valuable experience and develop leadership skills, besides giving them the visibility that makes further leadership roles possible.

The Budget Process. How an association allocates its funds is more than symbolic; it can have a real impact on what is accomplished. Budgetary procedures and decisions that promote affirmative action goals may take several forms. First, there are opportunities to spend money for the direct support of related programs (for example, through workshops and publications). Professional associations need to ask themselves whether funds are earmarked for programs that directly promote affirmative action goals. Second, the budgeting process itself may require that an affirmative action statement accompany any budget proposals. Those reviewing and approving budget requests may ask how each budget entity plans to implement affirmative action policies and practices. Will committees, boards, and targeted audiences be representative of women and racial/ethnic minority populations? Third, each budget entity could be asked to delineate specific programs or efforts to promote cultural diversity. It is easy for a bureaucratic organization to establish policies and procedures that are hardly more than words on paper, and it is easy to get caught up in quotas and proportions; but tying affirmative action goals to the budgeting process can give possible sanctions a real bite. Having affirmative action goals delineated and supported reduces the possibility of mere lip service to these important efforts.

Election-Slate Decisions. Gender- and race-balanced election slates make a readily visible statement to all association members: prospective association leaders are of both genders and all races. This statement establishes the possibility of clear role models for new association members, so that they will see that it is realistic for them, regardless of gender or race, to work toward leadership roles in their future professional activities. It may not be possible, or even advisable, for all slates to be balanced in each year, but it is important that such balance be evident over a reasonable period of time.

If, in determining election slates, those responsible find it difficult to offer balance, this difficulty can be a clue that work needs to be done at several levels, ranging from membership campaigns to committee appointments. It is important that candidates be truly viable and have respectable credentials matching the needs of the positions for which they are candidates, but this will be impossible if opportunities for leadership experiences have not been provided throughout the association's organizational structure and in all its activities.

Honors and Awards. Most associations present annual awards and grants for professional accomplishments, including awards for research and service. Recognition of this sort can be used to support the goals of affirmative action and cultural diversity. Special awards can be designed for researchers who conduct investigations related to cultural diversity (for example, relationship of ethnicity to college students' development, or gender and its relationship to career development). As appropriate, awards can also be earmarked for women and minorities. Similar service awards can be given to institutions or persons who design and evaluate intervention programs to increase and take advantage of cultural diversity on campus. Too much student affairs research has simply surveyed students' and faculty's opinions; much more is needed that provides educators with a deeper understanding of students and more insight into which intervention programs work, and why. Honors, awards, and special grants are excellent ways to encourage stimulating and useful research and program development.

Educational Programming

Educational programming is a natural activity of higher education associations, but attending to affirmative action goals requires special attention. It is helpful to give careful consideration to the content and purpose of the programming and to the delivery methods used.

Content and Purpose of Programming. Earlier chapters have provided the framework for broad-based educational programming—consideration of the rationale, history, and legal aspects of affirmative action. It is essential that these dimensions be dealt with continually, for two reasons: there are continually changing perspectives, as well as changes in laws and available data, and professional associations have a constant influx of new members. Unfortunately, it is naive to assume that all new association members are familiar with the issues related to sexism and racism, and it would be a grave mistake to assume any awareness on their part of the history of events within their individual professional specialties. If ignorance is prevalent, complacency cannot be far behind, and this is true not only for student affairs professionals but also for others in higher education. Students and faculty alike, for example, undoubtedly become familiar with historical facts in American history courses and with political and legal facts in government and political science courses, but how knowledgeable are they about what has happened historically in higher education and, particularly, in their own specialties?

Chapters One and Two emphasize the necessity of dealing with one's own philosophy and feelings about affirmative action goals. Knowledge and information about racism and sexism are necessary but insufficient to ensure the attitudinal and behavioral changes that must occur if affirmative action goals are to be truly accomplished. Deep and deep-seated negative feelings or ambivalence may exist even in the professionals who are most sincerely committed to these goals. These feelings may not rise to the surface when affirmative action goals are dealt with in the abstract, or when the individual's life is not directly touched, but only when the individual or a close friend or associate is being affected by a practice (say, in hiring or promotion) motivated by an affirmative action goal. A parallel set of feelings may also arise in the person who has obtained a position by what appears to be primarily an affirmative action based on gender or race. These feelings must be confronted in any consideration of educational programming related to affirmative action. Therefore, an integral aspect of decisions about topics for educational programming must concern the time to be spent and the methods used to help professionals examine their feelings about affirmative action.

Methods of Delivering Educational Programming. Almost any delivery method is appropriate and accessible to professional organizations, including conventions, workshops and publications, and lobbying.

Conventions. National and regional meetings are major showcase events for most professional associations in higher education. Convention programs show association members where the profession has been and provide a forum for discussion about where the profession is headed. Convention programming provides abundant educational opportunities for promoting affirmative action goals. Choices of major and featured speakers provide opportunities for displaying diversity among the speakers. Programs that focus on the needs of an increasingly diverse student body can receive high priority for selection.

Workshops and Publications. Not every association member can attend national conventions, and even those who do attend cannot go to all program sessions. Traveling workshops that have an appropriate blend of theory and instruction can be sponsored and designed for on-site campus delivery by experienced, knowledgeable professionals. Their focus can range from recruitment to retention, and proved model programs for dealing with racism and sexism on campus can be presented. Workshops provide opportunities for close interaction and personalizing of material.

Thus, host institutions (or regional participants) are able to obtain information that can be translated into local programs and practices.

Not every campus can host a workshop, but staffs have access to professional journals and newsletters, which too seldom serve as vehicles for discussing campus concerns. Professional associations can encourage editors to explore ways of publishing special issues that deal with affirmative action goals, or they can promote consideration of special sections of publications that highlight related articles and commentary. Professional associations also need to explore ways of encouraging members to form groups or organize staff meetings around journal articles. Too often, professionals rely on what they feel or believe, without sufficient support from the latest research (of course, this fact also implies the need for researchers and editors to make sure that material is readable and useful).

Lobbying. With the recent tendency of the Supreme Court to restrict affirmative action efforts, changes in legislation will probably become an increasingly important route for persons concerned about such issues as employment bias (Lee, 1989). Professional associations have the potential for being a powerful lobbying force at the state and national levels. Government-relations committees can provide professional associations with mechanisms (phone networks, letter-writing campaigns) for responding quickly to proposed legislation and, although this would be difficult, could even engage in consultation on proposed legislation.

Conclusion

Student affairs offices on college campuses have a reasonably good record of providing greater access for women and minorities to significant leadership positions on campus (Rickard, 1985; Rickard and Clement, 1984). Studies have found, however, that most women in administrative positions are single (Moore and Sagaria, 1982); that proportionally more men are chief student affairs officers by comparison with other men in director positions than is the case among women chief student affairs officers by comparison with other women directors (Rickard, 1985); and that institutional type is related to minority representation. A conservative conclusion is that much more needs to be done all along the career ladder, from admissions to training to hiring and promotion.

Ms. Blandina Cardenas Ramirez, director of the American Council on Education's Office of Minority Concerns, notes how important mentoring will be if the pool of minority faculty is to be increased significantly, and she also says that "at risk" students who "make it to the college door" need to be examined as much for their potential contributions as for their special needs (cited in Magner, 1989). For professional associations, taking care of their own houses with respect to equity issues is certainly a major challenge and responsibility, as is the burden that this effort may place on their budgets. Nevertheless, professional student affairs associations must engage enthusiastically in this effort and do their best to extend their influence. Their members have expertise in mentoring and human development, with a focus on the potential growth of students, staff, and faculty. Ms. Ramirez's challenge is one that student affairs professional associations and their individual members have repeatedly acknowledged and met, with some success. Now is not the time to stop.

References

Lee, B. A. "Recent Supreme Court Ruling Could Disrupt or Halt Affirmative Action Recruiting and Hiring in Academe." *Chronicle of Higher Education,* June 28, 1989, pp. B1, B3.

Magner, D. K. "Civil Rights Panelist Heads American Council's Minority Affairs Office." *Chronicle of Higher Education,* July 19, 1989, p. A3.

Moore, K. M., and Sagaria, M. D. "Differential Job Change and Stability Among Academic Administrators." *Journal of Higher Education,* 1982, *53,* 501-513.

Rickard, S. T. "The Chief Student Affairs Officer: Progress Toward Equity." *Journal of College Student Personnel,* 1985, *26,* 5-10.

Rickard, S. T., and Clement, L. M. "The Director of Admissions: Progress Toward Equity for Women and Minorities." *Journal of College Admissions,* 1984, *104,* 24-27.

Robert D. Brown is past president of the American College Personnel Association and past editor of the Journal of College Student Development. *He is the Carl A. Happold Distinguished Professor of Educational Psychology at the University of Nebraska–Lincoln.*

Responsibility for investing in affirmative action must be shared by all service and academic segments of a college or university and, more realistically, by society in general.

Investing in Affirmative Action: Everyone's Responsibility

J. Manuel Casas

During the last three decades, the major responsibility for setting affirmative action goals, developing policy, and implementing programs in most colleges and universities was largely relegated to offices under the administrative direction of student personnel services and, most frequently, to units aptly named "Economic Opportunity Programs" or "Student Affirmative Action." Student personnel services, mostly working through these units, accepted that responsibility and invested ever increasing resources, time, and energy to recruit and retain significant numbers of the growing proportion of racial/ethnic minority students who are finishing high school. In fact, according to a recent study conducted by the American Council on Education (El-Khawas, 1989), eight out of ten colleges and universities report either "a lot" or "some" activity aimed at boosting minority undergraduate enrollment.

From the outset, in recognition of the need to approach affirmative action from a long-term and comprehensive perspective, programs were developed that placed their attention on various educational levels (elementary, junior high school, high school, college), focused on various target groups (students, parents, counselors), and involved various individuals (mainly from student personnel offices, but now and then from academic divisions and departments). For examples of such programs, see El-Khawas (1989).

Unfortunately, despite these programs and activities, racial/ethnic minorities continue to be significantly underrepresented in higher education. This fact is not unknown to most college and university administrators; 60 percent of colleges and universities rated themselves only fair or poor in recruiting black students, and two-thirds rated themselves equally low in recruiting Hispanic students (El-Khawas, 1989). As we saw in Chapter Four, most of these institutions would also have to rate themselves fair or poor in efforts to retain and eventually graduate these students.

In the past, the failure to boost minority enrollments generally resulted only in administrative admonishments, directed at specific student personnel offices, to "try harder next year." Now, however, the highly publicized racial/ethnic demographic changes that are occurring in this country (see Chapter One) and the educational, economic, and social implications associated with such changes (see Levin, 1985) are forcing colleges and universities to accept the fact that, for society's sake as well as for their own survival, they must take actions that go beyond admonishments. Furthermore, it is quite obvious that such actions can no longer be relegated solely to the realm of student personnel services. The fact is that educational affirmative action goals can be attained only through concerted and collaborative efforts that involve all service, academic, and administrative segments of colleges and universities—and, more realistically, through complementary efforts by society in general and in particular by individuals, organizations, and institutions that have the knowledge, resources, and power to expedite such efforts.

It is not possible here to discuss all these individuals, organizations, and institutions. Therefore, as an illustration, and as a provocation to thought and discussion, I shall discuss three entities that can play vital, if not pivotal, roles in affirmative action: the faculty, accreditation and funding committees, and corporations.

What follows are examples that can easily be adapted to complement, facilitate, or support affirmative action efforts. Some of the examples present programs designed for implementation at the very earliest levels of education, in diverse academic and nonacademic settings, and based on the belief that the ultimate success of affirmative action depends on early and comprehensive interventions; after all, according to Judy Jackson Pitts, former assistant dean at Cornell University, "If higher education is interested in the harvesting of minority students, we have to get in on the planting" (cited in Tifft, 1989). Furthermore, the "planting" should take place in the settings most amenable to the nurturance and development of the educational dreams and abilities of the minority child.

Faculty

Many individuals familiar with the governance structure of a college or university would say that the faculty holds the final decision-making power across all aspects and levels of campus life. Therefore, it goes without saying that a faculty willing to invest time, energy, and resources in affirmative action can have a tremendous impact on the success of such efforts. To have such an impact, the investment of the faculty need not be totally revolutionary. On the contrary, it can be limited to taking an integral part in ongoing programs, such as in the following activities:

- Visiting local elementary, junior high, and high schools to expose students to diverse fields and professions while also motivating and encouraging students to work toward admission to the colleges and universities of their choice
- Serving as the college or university "godparents" to specific high schools and working in this capacity as advisers or friends to students interested in going on to a college or a university
- Offering short-term tutorials and classes on popular topics at local high schools or on college or university campuses
- Once students have submitted applications for admission, personally contacting a designated number of them by mail or phone, to maintain their interest and motivation, and, once the students are enrolled, serving as informal advisers or friends.

Faculty members can also expedite and streamline affirmative action efforts by developing their own effective programs:

- Carrying out research projects on local noncollege-age minority students, and designing such projects from a pragmatic perspective, so that findings can be easily understood and used to the benefit of local communities
- Submitting funding proposals through racial/ethnic minority–oriented nonprofit organizations (day-care centers, community centers, local schools, hospitals), so that money allotted for overhead expenses can be directly channeled into maintaining or improving the educational or other services provided by such organizations
- Actively recruiting and admitting racial/ethnic minority students into graduate programs in which they are underrepresented, supporting them, and serving as formal mentors, to ensure their successful and timely completion of graduate programs
- In collaboration with appropriate student personnel offices (especially those in charge of financial aid), offering academic internships and research-training mentorships for upper-division minority students; working closely with appropriate administrative offices to recruit and retain racial/ethnic minority faculty; and using a commonsense approach to developing a system for rewarding departments with additional faculty positions, research funds, or space, while withholding such resources from departments that fail to reach realistic goals (with emphasis for distributing resources on reaching goals, and not on fruitless effort)

• Taking steps to link affirmative action with academic excellence, through the development of an all-encompassing multiethnic curriculum.

Accreditation and Funding Committees

Professional organizations are in a powerful position to affect affirmative action. Nowhere is this fact more apparent than in accreditation and funding.

With respect to accreditation, professional organizations frequently have the final say on which universities or professional schools are given the seal of approval to train students entering a specific profession. Therefore, it goes without saying that affirmative action related to students and curricula would be given a tremendous boost if accreditation committees within professional organizations would do the following things:

• Require students applying to graduate and professional schools to have taken a specified number of designated multiethnic-based courses
• Make accreditation contingent on provision and nonelective offering of a designated number of multiethnic-based courses (like other required courses, these would be determined by accreditation or curriculum committees within each organization)
• Make accreditation contingent on the existence of specific recruitment, admission, and support programs for minority students
• Make accreditation contingent on equitable proportions of minority students and minority faculty in graduate programs.

Funding (from whatever source) for training and research, when the money is channeled through a professional organization, should also be made contingent on compliance with criteria similar to those described for accreditation.

Corporations

Aware of changing racial/ethnic demographics, corporations are heeding the warnings of economists (for example, Levin, 1985) and have come to realize that minorities are destined to play a very significant role in the continued economic development of this country. Many of these corporations are beginning to accept responsibility for investing their resources and exerting their influence to support ongoing educational affirmative action (scholarships, internships, summer work programs). More important, many of these corporations have taken the initiative to develop their own programs, designed for use in diverse socioeducational and work settings and, from a proactive perspective, directed at children who are at various developmental and educational levels. The following examples provide a brief overview of innovative corporate efforts (see Cordtz, 1989) that merit serious consideration for replication by other corporations:

- The chief executive officer of Honeywell heads an early-development pilot program in Minneapolis called "Success by 6," which provides a variety of special educational services to preschool-age children. This program operates in an area where 90 percent of the neighborhood's poor children are under the age of eighteen.
- In Miami, the American Bankers Insurance Group established what is called a "satellite learning center" at its headquarters. The company spent $350,000 for the facilities, and it budgets $60,000 a year for maintenance. The Dade County School System provides teachers, books, and equipment for forty children in kindergarten and first grade.
- In Prince George's County, Maryland, an educational partnership program was developed that, among other things, provides workplace schools near employment centers and offers care to the children of working parents, as well as comprehensive year-round services to at-risk youth.
- In Santa Barbara, California, the PEP-SI Program was able to get the school district, the business community, and the local campus of the University of California to pool their resources and expertise and provide a counseling, tutorial, and social skills–building program for minority students.

Conclusion

The need to attain affirmative action goals is so great that the responsibility for investing in relevant efforts must be shared by society in general and especially by individuals, organizations, and institutions that have the resources and the power to expedite such efforts. The education of all children is of such national importance that all levels of government must assume active leadership in affirmative action. If this country is to avoid the catastrophic social and economic consequences that may result from the failure to educate all its children, it cannot tolerate for very long the indifference or antagonism toward affirmative action that recent presidential administrations and the Supreme Court have demonstrated (see Chapter Three). Finally, some will argue that, with federal and state budgetary constraints and the critical state of our economy, additional investment in educational affirmative action is not very realistic. In reply to this argument, I shall take the liberty of paraphrasing Derek Bok (cited in Cordtz, 1989, p. 46): if you think investing in educational affirmative action is expensive, try ignorance.

References

Cordtz, D. "Dropouts: Retrieving America's Labor Lost." *Financial World*, 1989, *158*, 7, 36–46.

El-Khawas, E. *Campus Trends, 1989.* Washington, D.C.: American Council on Education, 1989.
Levin, H. *The State Youth Initiatives Project.* Philadelphia: Public/Private Ventures, 1985.
Tifft, S. "The Search for Minorities." *Time,* Aug. 21, 1989, pp. 64–65.

J. Manuel Casas is associate professor in the Counseling Psychology Program at the University of California–Santa Barbara. He is also the senior associate of JMC & Associates, a consulting firm that specializes in developing and implementing affirmative action training programs.

Tomorrow's affirmative action requires sharp planning by today's student affairs educators.

Affirmative Action: The Second Step

Doris J. Wright

At this writing, America is celebrating the twentieth anniversary of the first manned lunar landing. During ceremonies commemorating that event, President Bush pledged his commitment to a manned space flight to Mars, a project that will require the development of a space station on the moon. This pledge by the president represents yet another step—an important step for America and for the world, by any technological yardstick—in our efforts to assume leadership in space exploration and space technology. It also raises several questions relevant to our current discussion of affirmative action. Who will take that first step on Mars, that "one giant step"—A black or Hispanic woman? Will the space station's team include a Native American or an American Samoan among its technicians? What if we should discover new "peoples" in our exploration? How will they be assured of equal access to our high-tech Martian colleges and lunar universities?

Science fiction, you say? Are you certain? I am not. Space exploration cannot help bringing new challenges to the dilemma of equal access and affirmative action for America's peoples, whether they reside on the moon, on Mars, or in Milwaukee. We must plan today for these inevitable aspects of affirmative action tomorrow.

Throughout this volume, two themes have been clear. First, higher education's student populations are increasingly diverse, and with these shifts in student demographics comes the challenge to maintain equal access for all future American collegians, whether of African, European, Asian, Mexican, Spanish, or indigenous ancestry. Second, the structure and concepts of affirmative action are changing in response to recently decided and yet-to-be-decided Supreme Court rulings. These conceptual and court-created shifts will require colleges and universities to define new mechanisms for guaranteeing equal access. These themes place institutions in a perplexing position. While institutions may hold firmly to the moral imperative of providing equal opportunity for all who desire education and whose talents dictate it, they find themselves woefully unequipped to do so. Colleges and universities simply must face a harsh reality: in order to remain competitive, committed, conscientious learning environments, they must create and adopt equitable, innovative methods and means suitable not only to the recruiting but also to the educating of minorities and women.

More than thirty years of legal, political, and street battles for equal access to education—all initiated since the benchmark *Brown* v. *Topeka Board of Education* Supreme Court decision—have led much of the public, and virtually all its minority citizens, to expect leadership from higher education in championing equal access and affirmative action. This generation of minority students (as well as its parents) *expects* to have access to all the best college resources available; anything less seriously shortchanges them and the rest of American society.

While the philosophical principles of equal access and affirmative action used by educators and legal "gurus" of the past are still valid, the strategies and techniques of putting those principles into practice must be updated. Higher education cannot continue to employ the same strategies it used during the turbulent 1960s to ensure access to colleges in the year 2000. Administrators must develop new means of ensuring equal access to higher education, whether on the moon or in a floating "college at sea" for sailors patrolling Middle Eastern waters. To do this, we must ask many questions: What is true parity, in terms of the academic potential of ethnic minorities, women, persons with disabilities, and others? How will institutions distribute educational resources equitably? What must be changed, invented, and overcome? The search for answers often leads to yet more questions and to other areas that must be reconsidered and restructured.

Financial Exigencies

What happens to affirmative action when a staff position is lost, when hiring is frozen, or when operating budgets are cut because of financial shortfalls? What plans do institutions have for affirmatively and equitably managing layoffs or reductions in force and surviving staff hiring freezes? The answers to these and all too many other financial concerns must be examined in the context of affirmative action. Just as firefighters, emergency-room professionals, and law-enforcement officials prepare for handling emergencies and disasters, so must our colleges and universities begin to prepare for crises, such as financial shortfalls. They should examine procedures for enforcing affirmative action during financial emergencies, and they should have contingency plans in the event of these emergencies. Such planning could take the form of administrative or managerial exercises for department heads, deans, or vice-presidents during beginning-of-year planning retreats. These exercises could be extended later to other managers through staff development activities.

Personnel Shortages

Chapters Four and Five prompt some uncomfortable conclusions. Even if departments were completely committed to affirmative action and extremely aggressive in recruiting minorities, there would still be a shortage of minority professionals in several academic disciplines. The supply of minorities entering and graduating from our institutions is simply not sufficient to fill the many vacancies.

Add to that reality the fact that faculty shortages exist in nursing and education and among teaching scientists and engineers at nonresearch institutions, to cite just a few areas. As colleges look for ways to remedy these personnel shortfalls, how will affirmative action enter into the equation? Is there any risk that the "answer" will be to reinstate the "business as usual" establishment of not so long ago, a white male technocracy? The challenge of dealing with this shortage is complex, encompassing a multitude of political, demographic, and social factors, but it is one for which we must plan now, to prevent a more serious situation in the future. The solutions to these complicated problems must be sought long before we see applicants' résumés on our desks, even as early as those applicants' primary school years. Among minorities, such early "seeding" is essential to the timely creation of the high-tech educators, teaching scientists, and student affairs practitioners who will be so necessary in the future.

Consumer-Oriented Affirmative Action

Another area for administrators to examine is how student constituencies access and use campus resources, especially those within student services. While none of the court cases cited in this volume has alleged discrimination or bias against campus "consumers," or students, it is the wise administrator who studies students' service utilization in the context of equal access and affirmative action. Is it problematic that a campus may have a 10 percent black enrollment but that those consumers participate in college government (elected or appointive) at the rate of only 2 percent and constitute only 0.5 percent of students using the counseling center? Is it troublesome that blacks on the same campus comprise 35 percent of all referrals for discipline?

One often hears that "minority students utilize *our* student services at the same rate at which they enroll in our institution." If that is true, is this participation rate acceptable to student affairs professionals? What does equal access to student resources mean, if one group continually fails to participate in certain student services and is disproportionately represented in another? Is there discrimination or restriction of access to any support service? Is the enrollment rate of the general student population a realistic benchmark for measuring equal access to campus services? The answers to these and many other questions raise (or resurrect) some intriguing questions for student affairs practitioners.

Campus services may have different patterns of participation across minority groups, women, and persons with disabilities. For example, when it comes to alumni groups, endowment programs, college or departmental planned-giving activities, or discipline-specific honor societies, minorities may participate less frequently than others, but the reasons for this lower participation rate are unclear. Is there some bias or restricted access to these resources, or are there administrative or social customs that are offensive or at least unappealing to minorities? Colleges and universities can extend their esprit de corps for affirmative action if they attend to the manner in which students choose to participate in academic and social-support activities.

Endowment-Oriented Affirmative Action

There has been no discussion in this volume about the importance of affirmative action in alumni and endowment offices and in related planned-giving activities. The professional literature contains little discussion about minorities' involvement in (or exclusion from) alumni associations, departmental or college fund-raising activities, or college endowment associations. If universities are genuinely committed to equal access, however, then administrators must begin to ask how minorities participate in campuswide endowment and fund-raising activities because affirmative action in the future must extend to helping minority alumni reinvest their resources in their schools in ways mutually advantageous to alumni and institutions.

As alumni directors and others examine the procedures and policies for making financial contributions to institutions, they must consider how students will benefit from these contributions. Is it appropriate to designate minority-only funds, contributions whose beneficiaries will be minority student services or minority scholarships? What about the donor who wishes to give money obtained from South African investments, when the Black Students' Association has spoken out in favor of divestiture of the institution's funds from such investments? Must all contributions to an institution be shown to be free of any association with prejudice or bias? If a radical white-supremacist group decided to contribute to a minority scholarship program, should the institution accept this money? Those in charge of planned-giving programs must examine how legal and philosophical principles of affirmative action affect them and their donors, in order to develop practices and policies that are financially sound and equitable.

Reducing Tokenism

Institutions that are serious about affirmative action and equal access must end the practice of recruiting or hiring only one minority professional. The phenomenon of tokenism is seldom mentioned in the professional literature, but it is a hard reality for minority and women professionals. *Tokenism* refers to the practice of aggressively recruiting minorities or women for one staff position, hiring a minority or female professional (often for a designated minority position), and then failing or neglecting to maintain a diverse pool of applicants for subsequent vacancies. By failing to recruit minorities with the same energy as before, departments communicate a very discouraging message: "We have our minority. Why do we need to go through all that again? Isn't one enough for now?" By inference, the minority professional is perceived as having been hired on the basis of minority status, rather than for his or her qualifications and expertise.

Whether this practice is planned or accidental, real or perceived, it is troublesome to student groups, professional associations, governing boards, legislatures, and alumni because it gives the appearance of racial discrimination. This perception creates image problems for institutions and can undermine institutional efforts to be affirmative and equitable. Perhaps the most devastating aspect of this practice is the message it gives to minority professionals: "We value your minority status because it keeps us in compliance with affirmative action rules and out of trouble with the vice-president." Tokenism fails to affirm the rich talent that minority professionals have, and it ignores the importance of campus diversity in general.

If colleges and universities are genuinely committed to the spirit and practice of affirmative action and equal access for minorities and women, then corrective action is in order. Administrators should examine their minority hiring practices over five to ten years, to see if tokenism has occurred. If it has, corrective action is necessary to ensure that every vacancy has an ethnic- and gender-diverse applicant pool. If that is not possible, then administrators must know why their applicant pools fail to reflect the general population's diversity, and they must seek consultation and advice to correct this organizational deficiency. Tokenism restricts equal access and sabotages affirmative action, with consequent losses that higher education can ill afford, now or in the future.

Affirmative Education

Institutions that are serious about achieving academic excellence and that are committed to affirmative action must redefine their academic missions.

For tomorrow's educators, craftspersons, politicians, technicians, and scientists to be trained for pluralistic workplaces, academic excellence must be achieved in a multiethnic context. These new academic demands require affirmative action to be introduced into the classroom and related to the core learning process. I call this practice *affirmative education*.

Affirmative education implies that society can expand its knowledge base if learning and education occur in a pluralistic environment and if instructional practices embrace diversity of content, learning styles, instructional methods, and evaluation devices. Affirmative education, in contrast to the manner in which we now educate our students, respects and rewards the richness of talent to be found in a multiethnic classroom or laboratory.

Is this a revolutionary idea? Hardly. Astin (1985) and the Commission on Minority Participation in Education and American Life (1988) have proposed similar ideas for classroom diversity. Colleges' adoption of affirmative education puts to rest the inequities and biases inherent in the white male–normed, monolinguistic instructional process that we have used too long in higher education. Affirmative action is incomplete if we continue to allow prejudice and bias in our classrooms, laboratories, and faculties. Efforts to recruit and retain ethnic minorities and other disenfranchised students are undermined if they are invited to campus only to be greeted by prejudice in the classroom. We have affirmative action policies to manage discrimination in employment, recruiting, promotion, and enrollment— everywhere but in the classroom.

Colleges and universities on the cutting edge must link affirmative action with academic excellence, reinforce affirmative education in academic support services, and reward faculty for moving toward such goals. The potential outcomes of affirmative education are many. For students, the discovery of new problem-solving options and the evolution of innovative critical-thinking skills become possible; for institutions, the creation of dynamic instructional methods is a logical outgrowth. Creating an academic climate in which diverse minds can flourish and develop will benefit society: when diversity is fused with culture, innovative solutions to problems, new critical-thinking skills, and novel variations on age-old and new social issues are encouraged. Academic ideas are translated into innovative applications in industry, science, and medicine and may contribute to more rapid solutions to such human dilemmas as drug abuse and domestic violence. Connecting educational diversity with affirmative action makes possible, and even probable, solutions that we cannot even imagine.

Reducing Color-Blindness

An important next step in affirmative action for colleges and universities is to examine the institutional costs of color-blindness on campus. Future college students will increasingly be minorities and women (Commission on Minority Participation in Education and American Life, 1988). Likewise, the work force early in the next century will reflect similar ethnic and gender diversity. It would be ridiculous as well as impractical for colleges and universities to educate these students as if they were white monolingual males—the model college students of the past. Because student and faculty demographics are likely to change drastically in the future, color-blind and class-bound educational strategies may run in to head-on conflict with a pluralistic campus population. Color-blindness is just that: eyes (and minds) are closed to the richness and unique value of diversity. Institutions will serve themselves (and their future investments) best by reexamining the merits of color-blindness in classrooms, dormitories, and student services, as well as in affirmative action policies and guidelines. Color-blindness is self-limiting for the student and the institution alike, and it prepares neither one for a pluralistic twenty-first century.

The courts still seem undecided about the merits of such race-conscious strategies as preferential treatment and uncertain about how colleges should use color-blind legal remedies. Nevertheless, the verdict is in on the social and educational merits of adopting a color-blind affirmative action strategy. Tomorrow's college students, their parents, and future donors will not tolerate the institution that does not acknowledge and reward pluralism and diversity. Colleges and universities must reexamine the strategies they employ to guarantee equal access for minorities and women, and they must especially challenge color-blind policies and practices.

Conclusion

The future of affirmative action for colleges and universities is largely uncharted territory. For more than three decades, institutions have lagged or resisted in assuming total responsibility for designing, monitoring, and managing affirmative action policies and equal-access interventions. A variety of social, political, and economic reasons have contributed to this resistance, not the least of which has been institutions' own discriminatory practices. Future directions (which will extend into space, if President Bush's promise is realized) will require America's colleges and universities to assume full responsibility for ensuring equal access to all future students. I do not advocate a return to states' rights or to the kind of retrenchment in civil rights that the doctrine of states' rights involved in the 1950s and 1960s; I do encourage colleges and universities to grow up, and to end their dependence on such external entities as the federal government and the courts to set affirmative action directions. American colleges and universities are quite capable of assuming such leadership, now and in the future.

Colleges and universities must meet the challenges posed by affirmative action now if they are to survive and grow in the twenty-first century and beyond. Of course, this responsibility means that institutions must take a risk and hope that adherence to egalitarian concepts will entail organizational benefits. This risk, on the surface, is a low-level challenge, and yet it is one that most institutions, at least until quite recently have been unwilling to take.

The next step in affirmative action is a giant leap. Success for colleges in the years ahead will require them to fuse the goals of academic excellence and equal access, thereby introducing affirmative action principles into classroom instruction and equal access into other areas. The classroom, with its emphasis on such hallowed arenas as curricula, teaching methods, academic advising, support services, and so forth, presents itself as the last affirmative action frontier to conquer. Institutions must reexamine their policies to ensure that their actions will remain congruent with legal precedents, social imperatives, and consumer demands. For example, institutions may need to revise their professional codes of ethics to include diversity and equal access as valued organizational norms.

Two realities remain noteworthy. First, the college campus will always be diverse and heterogeneous. Even if institutions decide to raise their academic standards in order to screen or weed out students (in the hope of eliminating minorities), they will still have some minority students. Second, tomorrow's diverse students, their taxpaying parents, and the equally diverse work force will not tolerate business as usual—a racist, sexist, ageist, homophobic, white male-dominated college learning environment. Like it or not, colleges and their administrators must accept the inevitable; to fail to accept these realities is institutionally self-defeating and self-abasing.

American colleges and universities remain the premier institutions of higher learning in the world (and, we presume, in any other). To remain at this pinnacle will mean to embrace diversity and equal access in an affirmative education framework, with the outcome of academic excellence for all.

References

Astin, A. W. *Achieving Educational Excellence: A Critical Assessment of Priorities and Practices in Higher Education.* San Francisco: Jossey-Bass, 1985.

Commission on Minority Participation in Education and American Life. *One Third of a Nation.* Washington, D.C.: American Council on Education, Education Commission of the States, 1988.

Doris J. Wright is program director for consultation services and staff psychologist at the Counseling and Mental Health Center of the University of Texas–Austin.

Summary points are highlighted, and a list of additional sources is provided.

Summary and Additional Sources of Information

Joseph G. Ponterotto, Diane E. Lewis, Robin Bullington

If one succinct message were extracted from this volume, it would be this: affirmative action is not someone else's responsibility; it is yours. Affirmative action on campus will not succeed unless all campus personnel and students understand the rationale and justification for such policies. To enlighten the university environment about the subtle realities of continuing racism and sexism, off campus and on, an intensified awareness program should be implemented on all campuses. Such education could take the form of a required course on cultural diversity for all incoming students at all levels, and regardless of background and experience; training and available consultation for all faculty and administrators; and cultural pluralism in course curricula.

Colleges and universities must take the initiative in affirmative action. They must understand which implementation procedures are within the law, and they must employ creative, long-term strategies. Equally important will be universities' ability to work with off-campus constituencies: professional organizations, funding agencies, the business sector, and diverse minority communities.

Changing a historically and traditionally white, middle-class, male environment into one where all groups feel equally valued and wanted is a challenging and long-term task. "Quick fixes" will succeed only in the short run, if at all. Detailed and flexible ten-to-twenty-year intervention plans should be established by all predominantly white colleges and universities. The committees and boards that develop these plans should be multicultural in composition, representing the campus (students, faculty, and administrators), elementary and secondary education, the community at large, and the business sector. Colleges and universities need not await signals from the Bush administration or the Supreme Court to act affirmatively. Educational institutions develop and educate the future leaders of our nation, and it is up to institutions to ensure that all segments of the population are adequately represented among future leaders.

Understandably, most colleges and universities have a long way to go in their efforts toward pluralism. The annotated bibliography that follows should help in long-range planning.

Books

Cox, P. N. *Employment Discrimination.* New York: Garland Law Publishing, 1988.

This volume provides a critical analysis of diverse aspects of employment-discrimination law.

Dreyfuss, J. D., and Lawrence, C. *The Bakke Case: The Politics of Inequality.* San Diego, Calif.: Harcourt Brace Jovanovich, 1979.

This is a thorough and highly readable account of the case that brought the so-called reverse-discrimination question before the Supreme Court.

Green, M. F. (ed.). *Minorities on Campus: A Handbook for Enhancing Diversity.* Washington, D.C.: American Council on Education, 1988.

This is a straightforward, suggestion-specific handbook on increasing cultural diversity at all levels of higher education. Sample programs are highlighted, and specific worksheets (for example, on longitudinal recruitment timetables) are presented. This is perhaps the single most helpful source available.

LaNoue, G. R., and Lee, B. A. *Academics in Court: The Consequences of Faculty Discrimination Litigation.* Ann Arbor: University of Michigan Press, 1987.

This work examines the effects of litigation on all involved parties—faculty, counsel, and employing institutions. Five detailed case studies are presented, and data from national surveys of faculty plaintiffs and university counsel are reviewed.

Nettles, M. T. (ed.). *Toward Black Undergraduate Student Equality in American Education.* Westport, Conn.: Greenwood Press, 1988.

This is an excellent overview of the current status of blacks in higher education. Coverage is given to academic and achievement issues and to contemporary barriers to higher education, as well as to the role of universities, the state, and the federal government in equality efforts.

Pearson, C. S., Shavlik, D. L., and Touchton, J. G. (eds.). *Educating the Majority: Women Challenge Tradition in Higher Education.* New York: Macmillan, 1989.

This comprehensive analysis of women in higher education—past, present, and future—is an enlightening presentation on campus diversity, learning environments shaped by women, and future directions needed in higher education.

Richardson, R. C., Jr., and Bender, L. W. *Fostering Minority Access and Achievement in Higher Education: The Role of Urban Community Colleges and Universities.* San Francisco: Jossey-Bass, 1987.

Based on two large-scale funded surveys, this book focuses on the underrepresentation of blacks and Hispanics in four-year institutions and highlights crucial elements of the "pipeline" from two-year colleges to four-year colleges and universities.

Taylor, C. A. *Effective Ways to Recruit and Retain Minority Students.* Madison, Wisc.: Praxis Publications, 1987.

This very practical guide offers specific steps for recruiting and retaining minority students. A retention model is presented, and seventeen crucial program components are assessed.

Articles and Special Reports

Clague, M. W. "The Affirmative Action Showdown of 1986: Implications for Higher Education." *Journal of College and University Law,* 1987, *14* (2), 171–257.

The author focuses on the three affirmative action cases that the Supreme Court heard during its 1985 term. Decisions and opinions of the justices are examined, and specific implications for higher education are emphasized.

Commission on Minority Participation in Education and American Life. *One-Third of A Nation.* Washington, D.C.: American Council on Education, Education Commission of the States, 1988.

This frequently discussed national report assesses the current status of minorities in education and employment, highlighting the social and economic implications of continued minority underrepresentation in higher education.

Coyle, M. "At the Court: Storm After the Calm!" *National Law Journal,* Oct. 3, 1988, pp. 1–26.

This article examines the 1988 Supreme Court term in light of the addition of Justice Kennedy and the creation of a conservative majority.

Morris, A. A. "Affirmative Action and 'Quota' Systems." *Education Law Reporter*, 1986, *28*, 1203-1235.

The article discusses definitional, philosophical, and moral issues in affirmative action policy. The author draws conclusions about and makes projections from the Supreme Court's apparent ambivalence in a number of civil rights cases.

Sowell, T. "*Weber* and *Bakke*, and the Presuppositions of Affirmative Action." *Wayne Law Review*, 1980, *26* (4), 1309-1336.

This challenge to the policies of preferential treatment reviews the development of affirmative action philosophy and processes.

University Committee on Minority Issues. *Building a Multiracial, Multicultural University Community.* Stanford, Calif.: University Committee on Minority Issues, Stanford University, 1989.

This is a comprehensive self-study of the representation of minorities on the Stanford campus and of the academic and social climate confronting racially diverse groups. The highly readable, well-organized report provides an excellent model for other predominantly white universities.

Weiss, R. J. "Affirmative Action: A Brief History." *Journal of Intergroup Relations*, 1987, *15* (2), 40-53.

This succinct political history of affirmative action notes the change in focus from the 1960s to the 1980s.

Joseph G. Ponterotto is associate professor of counseling and counseling psychology in the Division of Psychological and Educational Services, Graduate School of Education, Fordham University–Lincoln Center, New York.

Diane E. Lewis is a doctoral student in counseling psychology at Fordham University.

Robin Bullington is a doctoral student in counseling psychology at the University of Houston.

INDEX

Aaronson, E., 55, 58
Accreditation committees, role of, 86
Achenbaum, W. A., 9, 13
Adelman, R. W., 39, 42
Admissions, laws regarding, 30
Affirmative action, 1-2, 17-18, 95-96, 97-98; goals of, 5-6; history of, 18-19; implementation of, 73-96; legal issues of, 27-42; literature on, 98-100; philosophy of, 19-24; and student affairs administrators, 11-13, 24-25
Affirmative discrimination *See* Preferential treatment
Affirmative education, 93-94. *See also* Cultural diversity
Age Discrimination Act of 1975, 31
Ageism, 9. *See also* Elderly
Alumni, and affirmative action, 92
American Bankers Insurance Group, 87
American College Personnel Association of the American Association for Counseling and Development, 70-71
American Council on Education, 10-11, 47, 51, 52-53, 58, 63-66, 72, 83; Office of Minority Concerns of, 80
American Psychological Association, 9-10, 13; Scientific Directorate of, 40
Asian Americans, 46-54; in administration, 62-64; and faculty representation, 64-66. *See also* Racial/ethnic minorities
Assertiveness, 56
Association of American Colleges, 67, 68, 72
Astin, A. W., 7, 8, 13, 94, 96
Atkinson, D. R., 7, 8, 9, 13, 41, 42
At-risk students, 55
Attrition rates, of minorities, 10, 52-53; mitigation of, 53-54
Autonomy, 55

Bales, J., 39, 40, 42
Barr, M. J., 27, 42
"Barrioization," 67-68
Beckham, B., 54, 58
Beer, W. R., 19, 21, 24, 25
Bender, L. W., 7, 8, 10, 14, 51, 59, 99

Bernhardt, R., 70, 72
Bersoff, D. N., 39, 42
Betz, N. E., 8, 13
Black Americans, 46-54; in administration, 62-64; and faculty representation, 64-66. *See also* Minorities, Racial/ethnic minorities
Blackmun, Justice, 20
Bok, D., 21, 25, 87
Bowe, F., 9, 13
Brennan, Justice, 37-38, 40
Brimelow, P., 19, 25
Brown, R. D., 2-3, 73
Brown v. Topeka Board of Education, 90
Bush, President, 89, 95

Camara, W., 40
Campus climate, and minorities, 7, 53-58, 67-69. *See also* Cultural diversity
Campus housing, laws regarding, 30
Cancelli, A. A., 70, 72
Cardoza, J., 47, 58
Carter, President, 18
Casas, J. M., 2-3, 7, 10, 13, 14, 46, 56, 58, 73
Center for Leadership Development, 63
Chipman, S. F., 7, 13
City of Richmond v. J. A. Croson Co., 32, 33, 35, 36, 37, 43
Civil rights, 18; laws protecting, 27-31
Civil Rights Act of 1866, Sec. 1981, 28, 33, 36
Civil Rights Act of 1871, Sec. 1983, 29
Civil Rights Act of 1964, 18; Title VI, 29, 34, 36; Title VII, 29-30, 33-34, 35, 36, 39-41
Civil Rights Restoration Act of 1987, 31
Clague, M. W., 35, 37, 38, 40, 41, 42, 99
Clement, L. M., 80, 81
Clewell, B. C., 71, 72
Color-blind approach, 19-20, 94-95. *See also* Cultural diversity, Preferential treatment
Commission on Minority Participation in Education and American Life, 8, 10-11, 13, 47, 58, 94-95, 96, 99
Common good. *See* Social utility

101

ORDERING INFORMATION

NEW DIRECTIONS FOR STUDENT SERVICES is a series of paperback books that offers guidelines and programs for aiding students in their total development—emotional, social, and physical, as well as intellectual. Books in the series are published quarterly in Fall, Winter, Spring, and Summer and are available for purchase by subscription as well as by single copy.

SUBSCRIPTIONS for 1990 cost $42.00 for individuals (a savings of 20 percent over single-copy prices) and $56.00 for institutions, agencies, and libraries. Please do not send institutional checks for personal subscriptions. Standing orders are accepted.

SINGLE COPIES cost $13.95 when payment accompanies order. (California, New Jersey, New York, and Washington, D.C., residents please include appropriate sales tax.) Billed orders will be charged postage and handling.

DISCOUNTS FOR QUANTITY ORDERS are available. Please write to the address below for information.

ALL ORDERS must include either the name of an individual or an official purchase order number. Please submit your order as follows:
Subscriptions: specify series and year subscription is to begin
Single copies: include individual title code (such as SS1)

MAIL ALL ORDERS TO:
Jossey-Bass Inc., Publishers
350 Sansome Street
San Francisco, California 94104

FOR SALES OUTSIDE OF THE UNITED STATES CONTACT:
Maxwell Macmillan International Publishing Group
866 Third Avenue
New York, New York 10022

U.S. Postal Service

STATEMENT OF OWNERSHIP, MANAGEMENT AND CIRCULATION
Required by 39 U.S.C. 3685

1A. Title of Publication	1B. PUBLICATION NO.							2. Date of Filing
New Directions for Student Services	4	4	9	–	0	7	0	9/18/90

3. Frequency of Issue	3A. No. of Issues Published Annually	3B. Annual Subscription Price
Quarterly	Four (4)	$48 individual $70 institutional

4. Complete Mailing Address of Known Office of Publication (Street, City, County, State and ZIP+4 Code) (Not printers)

350 Sansome Street, San Francisco, CA 94104-1310

5. Complete Mailing Address of the Headquarters of General Business Offices of the Publisher (Not printer)

(above address)

6. Full Names and Complete Mailing Address of Publisher, Editor, and Managing Editor (This item MUST NOT be blank)
Publisher (Name and Complete Mailing Address)

Jossey-Bass Inc., Publishers
Editor (Name and Complete Mailing Address)

Margaret J. Barr, Sadler Hall, Texas Christian Univ., Fort Worth, TX 76129
Managing Editor (Name and Complete Mailing Address)

Steven Piersanti, President, Jossey-Bass Inc., Publishers (above address)

7. Owner (If owned by a corporation, its name and address must be stated and also immediately thereunder the names and addresses of stockholders owning or holding 1 percent or more of total amount of stock. If not owned by a corporation, the names and addresses of the individual owners must be given. If owned by a partnership or other unincorporated firm, its name and address, as well as that of each individual must be given. If the publication is published by a nonprofit organization, its name and address must be stated.) (Item must be completed.)

Full Name	Complete Mailing Address
Maxwell Communications Corp., plc	Headington Hill Hall Oxford OX30BW U.K.

8. Known Bondholders, Mortgagees, and Other Security Holders Owning or Holding 1 Percent or More of Total Amount of Bonds, Mortgages or Other Securities (If there are none, so state)

Full Name	Complete Mailing Address
same as above	same as above

9. For Completion by Nonprofit Organizations Authorized To Mail at Special Rates (DMM Section 423.12 only)
The purpose, function, and nonprofit status of this organization and the exempt status for Federal income tax purposes (Check one)

(1) ☐ Has Not Changed During Preceding 12 Months	(2) ☐ Has Changed During Preceding 12 Months	If changed, publisher must submit explanation of change with this statement.)

10.	Extent and Nature of Circulation (See instructions on reverse side)	Average No. Copies Each Issue During Preceding 12 Months	Actual No. Copies of Single Issue Published Nearest to Filing Date
A.	Total No. Copies (Net Press Run)	2000	2143
B.	Paid and/or Requested Circulation 1. Sales through dealers and carriers, street vendors and counter sales	254	235
	2. Mail Subscription (Paid and/or requested)	996	496
C.	Total Paid and/or Requested Circulation (Sum of 10B1 and 10B2)	1250	731
D.	Free Distribution by Mail, Carrier or Other Means Samples, Complimentary, and Other Free Copies	78	95
E.	Total Distribution (Sum of C and D)	1328	826
F.	Copies Not Distributed 1. Office use, left over, unaccounted, spoiled after printing	672	1317
	2. Return from News Agents	0	0
G.	TOTAL (Sum of E, F1 and 2—should equal net press run shown in A)	2000	2143

11. I certify that the statements made by me above are correct and complete	Signature and Title of Editor, Publisher, Business Manager, or Owner Larry Ishii Vice-President

PS Form 3526, Feb. 1989 (See instructions on reverse)

A